# start your podcas

## A REFERENCE GUIDE ON HOW TO START A PODCAST

### KRISTA WILLIAMS

2

*This book is dedicated to my mother, who always made me feel like I could do anything I put my mind to.*

# Chapter 1: Navigating the Vast Landscape of Podcasting

# 1.1 Introduction: Decoding the Essence of Podcasting

———

Welcome to the thrilling universe of podcasting—a captivating realm where audio narratives flourish, and creators connect with diverse audiences worldwide. This chapter serves as your gateway to this dynamic medium, unraveling the intricacies of podcasting. Let's not only define podcasting but also trace its evolution, explore its current popularity, and understand the motivations driving individuals, like yourself, to venture into the realm of podcast creation.

## 1.1.1 Unveiling the Essence of Podcasting

PODCASTING IS A DIGITAL odyssey, offering creators an innovative platform to deliver episodic audio content to a global audience. Unlike traditional broadcasting, podcasts provide a convenient, on-demand listening experience. This section will be our compass, guiding you through the foundational elements of podcasting and setting the stage for your immersive journey.

### *Podcasting's Transformative Impact*

Podcasting, in its essence, is a revolutionary medium that bridges the gap between storytellers and audiences. Unlike traditional forms of media, podcasts offer a unique and personalized listening experience. The podcasting landscape has grown exponentially, with millions of podcasts covering an extensive range of topics. There were more than 424 million podcast listeners worldwide in 2023, a notable increase from 274.8 million in 2019. Additionally, the industry is projected to grow to 464.7 million by the end of the year, accounting for 22% of all internet users.

### Podcasting as a Cultural Phenomenon

Turns out, it's an over 23 billion dollar industry as of 2023, but this growth is projected to increase to over 100 billion before 2030. This surge in podcast creation underscores the accessibility and appeal of the medium. With over 2.5 million active podcasts and 68 million episodes available across various platforms, podcasting has become a cultural phenomenon.

## Global Reach

One of the defining features of podcasting is its global reach. According to a report by Podcast Analytics Platform, podcasts are consumed in over 190 countries, transcending geographical boundaries. This global accessibility allows podcasters to connect with diverse audiences and share narratives that resonate on a universal level.

## On-Demand Listening

The on-demand nature of podcasting has contributed significantly to its popularity. Recent studies indicate that 62% of podcast listeners prefer on-demand content over scheduled broadcasts. This shift in consumer behavior aligns with the lifestyle of today's audience, who seek flexibility in their media consumption.

## Engagement Metrics

Podcasting platforms provide valuable metrics for creators to gauge audience engagement. On average, podcasts retain 80% of their audience throughout an episode, showcasing the captivation of listeners. Additionally, Edison Research indicates that 54% of podcast listeners are likely to follow through with a call-to-action mentioned in an episode, highlighting the active and engaged nature of the podcasting audience.

## Diverse Content Landscape

Podcasting caters to an extensive range of interests and niches. From business and technology to true crime and personal development, there's a podcast for everyone. The Podcast Genre Report reveals that 45% of podcasts fall under the categories of Technology, Business, and Society & Culture, reflecting the diversity within the podcasting landscape.

In essence, podcasting is not just a medium; it's a dynamic platform that empowers creators to share stories, insights, and expertise with a global audience. As we navigate through this guide, you'll gain the knowledge and skills needed to carve your niche in the expansive world of podcasting.

## 1.1.2 An Odyssey Through Time: The Growth and Popularity of Podcasts

TO APPRECIATE THE SIGNIFICANCE of podcasting, let's embark on a historical journey. From its modest origins in the early 2000s to its current status as a cultural phenomenon, the evolution of podcasts is nothing short of extraordinary. We'll delve into the factors fueling its meteoric rise and explore the diverse genres captivating millions of listeners globally.

### The Genesis of Podcasting

Podcasting's roots can be traced back to the early 2000s when a group of innovative thinkers sought to create a platform for on-demand audio content. It began as a niche hobby, with early adopters experimenting with the concept of downloadable audio files. The term "podcast" itself is a portmanteau of "iPod" and "broadcast," highlighting its association with Apple's iconic device and the idea of broadcasting content to a digital audience.

### The Pioneering Podcasts

Some of the earliest podcasts were created by tech enthusiasts and independent radio producers. These pioneers laid the foundation for the medium by exploring a wide range of topics, from tech news to storytelling. As the medium gained traction, more individuals and organizations recognized its potential, leading to the diverse podcasting landscape we see today.

### The Democratization of Audio

One of the most remarkable aspects of podcasting is its democratization of audio content. Unlike traditional radio and television, where gatekeepers controlled access to the airwaves, podcasting allows anyone with a microphone and a compelling idea to become a content creator. This democratization has given rise to a rich tapestry of voices, perspectives, and stories.

**From Niche to Mainstream**

The growth of podcasting has been nothing short of explosive. In the early days, podcasts were considered a niche form of media. However, as smartphones became ubiquitous and streaming platforms embraced podcasts, the medium transitioned from niche to mainstream. Today, podcasts cover an astonishing array of topics, and they attract audiences that rival traditional media outlets.

**The Podcasting Renaissance**

In recent years, we've witnessed a podcasting renaissance characterized by increased production quality, high-profile celebrity hosts, and substantial investments from media companies. This renaissance has propelled podcasting into a new era of creativity and innovation, further solidifying its place in the media landscape.

## 1.1.3 The Podcasting Ecosystem: A Digital Revolution

UNDERSTANDING PODCASTING goes beyond the act of recording and publishing. Platforms like Apple Podcasts, Spotify, and Google Podcasts serve as digital hubs connecting creators with their audiences. We'll explore how this democratization of broadcasting has empowered individuals to amplify their voices, sharing narratives that resonate across borders.

**The role of Podcasting Platforms**

Podcasting platforms are at the heart of the medium's distribution. They provide a centralized space for hosting, distributing, and promoting podcasts to a global audience. Apple Podcasts, with its pioneering role, played a significant part in popularizing podcasts, but it's just one player in a diverse ecosystem.

**Discoverability and Curation**

As the number of podcasts continues to grow, discoverability becomes a key challenge for both creators and listeners. Platforms employ algorithms and curated playlists to help listeners find content tailored to their interests. This has led to the rise of personalized recommendations and podcast discovery tools.

## Monetization Opportunities

Podcasting platforms have also introduced monetization features, allowing creators to earn income from their podcasts. From advertising and sponsorships to subscription models and listener support, podcasters have a range of options to sustain and grow their shows.

## Accessibility and Inclusivity

The digital nature of podcasting makes it accessible to a global audience. It transcends language barriers and geographical boundaries, enabling creators to reach listeners from diverse backgrounds. This inclusivity has given rise to podcasts in multiple languages and an array of niche topics.

⇨ **Multilingual Content:** Podcasting platforms have become a hub for content in various languages. Creators can produce podcasts in their native tongue, allowing them to connect with listeners worldwide. This diversity of languages enriches the podcasting landscape, making it truly global.

⇨ **Niche Topics and Diverse Voices:** Podcasting's inclusivity extends to the content itself. Creators are not limited by traditional media gatekeepers, which means that niche topics and underrepresented voices can thrive. Whether it's a podcast about indigenous cultures, a discussion of disability issues, or a deep dive into LGBTQ+ history, podcasting provides a platform for stories and perspectives that might not find a place in mainstream media.

⇨ **Accessibility Features**: Podcasting platforms often incorporate features to enhance accessibility. This includes options for closed captions or transcripts, making content more accessible to individuals with hearing impairments or those who prefer to read.

Additionally, podcast apps may have adjustable playback speeds, benefiting listeners who need more time to process spoken content.

⇨ **Global Connection**: Podcasting has the power to connect people globally, fostering cross-cultural understanding and appreciation. Listeners from different parts of the world can access and engage with content that broadens their horizons, exposes them to new ideas, and deepens their understanding of other cultures.

⇨ **Inclusivity Initiatives**: Many podcasters actively work to ensure their content is inclusive and representative. This might involve featuring diverse guests, discussing important social issues, or actively seeking out underrepresented voices in their niche. Inclusivity initiatives within the podcasting community are contributing to a more equitable and diverse media landscape.

In conclusion, podcasting's digital ecosystem has democratized content creation and consumption, allowing for greater accessibility and inclusivity. It has broken down barriers that once limited who could participate in media, opening the door to a diverse range of voices and perspectives. As podcasting continues to evolve, it has the potential to become even more inclusive, ensuring that everyone's story can be told and heard in this dynamic medium.

# 1.2 The Heartbeat of Podcasting: Discovering Your Motivations

———

Why does the prospect of starting a podcast appeal to you? This section delves into common motivations, encouraging you to reflect on your own aspirations and paving the way for a purpose-driven podcasting journey.

## 1.2.1 Share Your Passion: Crafting Sonic Narratives

ARE YOU DEEPLY PASSIONATE about a particular subject? Whether it's an obscure hobby, a niche interest, or a burning cause, podcasting provides an unparalleled canvas for enthusiasts to share their fervor. Let's explore how your podcast can become a dynamic platform to express your passion authentically, connecting with like-minded individuals worldwide.

### The Power of Passion

Passion fuels creativity, and it's a driving force behind many successful podcasts. When you're passionate about a subject, your enthusiasm shines through in your content. Listeners can sense your genuine interest, making them more likely to engage and return for more.

### Choosing Your Niche

Identifying your passion is the first step. Consider what topics, hobbies, or causes resonate deeply with you. Your podcast's niche should align with your passion and expertise. Don't be afraid to dive deep into subjects that truly matter to you.

### Authenticity Matters

One of the unique aspects of podcasting is its authenticity. Listeners appreciate hosts who are genuine and passionate. When you share your passion authentically, you build trust with your audience, creating a loyal following.

## 1.2.2 Building a Personal Brand: The Sonic Signature

IN THE DIGITAL AGE, personal branding is paramount. A podcast serves as a powerful tool for establishing and enhancing your personal brand. Let's discuss strategies for leveraging your podcast to showcase your expertise, connect with your audience on a personal level, and solidify your online presence.

### Your Podcast as a Branding Tool

Your podcast is an extension of yourself and your brand. The way you present your content, your style of communication, and the topics you choose all contribute to your personal brand. Consider how you want to be perceived by your audience.

### Consistency is Key

Consistency in your podcast's branding is crucial. This includes elements like your podcast's logo, intro music, and overall tone. A consistent brand helps listeners recognize your content across various platforms.

### Engaging with Your Audience

Your podcast provides a unique opportunity to engage with your audience. Encourage listener feedback, questions, and comments. Engaging with your audience builds a sense of community and strengthens your personal brand.

## 1.2.3 Community Connection: Beyond the Microphone

PODCASTING HAS THE magical ability to cultivate communities. By producing content that resonates with your target audience, you can create a tight-knit community around your podcast. Let's explore practical strategies for community building, engagement, and transforming your podcast into a vibrant, interactive space.

### Fostering Community Engagement

Your podcast can serve as a hub for discussions, interactions, and shared experiences. Encourage listeners to participate in your podcast's community, whether through social media groups, forums, or live events. Engaging with your audience outside of your episodes fosters a sense of belonging.

**Live Shows and Q&A Sessions**

Consider hosting live podcast episodes or Q&A sessions with your audience. Live interactions allow you to connect with your listeners in real-time, answer their questions, and receive immediate feedback.

**Collaborations and Listener Contributions**

Invite listeners to contribute content or ideas for your podcast. This not only involves your community but also provides fresh perspectives and keeps your content diverse and engaging.

## 1.2.4 Educational Opportunities: Sharing Knowledge Through Soundwaves

PODCASTING TRANSCENDS entertainment; it's an excellent medium for education. Whether you're imparting practical skills, sharing insights from your experiences, or hosting expert interviews, your podcast can become an educational beacon. Let's delve into the art of educational podcasting, offering guidance on structuring your content for maximum impact and reaching a diverse audience eager to learn.

**The Educational Podcasting Landscape**

Educational podcasts come in various forms, from tutorials and lectures to in-depth explorations of complex topics. Identify your educational niche and target audience to tailor your content effectively.

**Structured Content Delivery**

To ensure your educational content is engaging and effective, consider structured formats. Organize your episodes logically, provide clear explanations, and use storytelling techniques to make learning enjoyable.

**Expert Interviews and Insights**

Bringing experts onto your podcast can enhance its educational value. Expert interviews provide authoritative insights and diversify your content. Collaborating with knowledgeable guests adds credibility to your podcast.

By exploring these motivations, you'll not only find your unique voice in the podcasting world but also connect with an audience that shares your passions, values your personal brand, engages with your community, and benefits from your educational content. Your podcast will become a powerful tool for making a difference in your chosen field and fulfilling your podcasting dreams.

# 1.3 Charting the Course Ahead

As you embark on your podcasting journey, it's essential to have a roadmap that guides you through the diverse and exciting world of podcast creation. In this section, we'll lay out the structure of this book, explain how to make the most of it, introduce your podcasting toolkit, and help you prepare to dive into the thrilling world of podcasting.

## 1.3.1 The Structure of This Book

THIS BOOK IS DESIGNED to be your comprehensive guide to podcasting, from concept to execution. We've organized it into distinct sections and chapters, each focusing on a critical aspect of podcast creation. Here's an overview of what you can expect:

❖ **Chapter 1: Navigating the Vast Landscape of Podcasting** – You're currently in this chapter, where we've introduced you to podcasting, and explored its essence, motivations, and the potential it holds.

❖ **Chapter 2: Crafting Your Podcast Concept** – In this chapter, we'll guide you through the process of defining your podcast's purpose, target audience, format, and niche. It's the foundation upon which your podcast will be built.

❖ **Chapter 3: Planning Your Podcast Episodes** – Here, we'll dive into the art of episode planning. You'll learn how to structure your episodes, create engaging content, and outline your scripts or talking points.

❖ **Chapter 4: Recording and Production** – This chapter covers the technical aspects of podcasting, from selecting the right equipment and software to recording and editing your episodes for professional-quality results.

❖ **Chapter 5: Branding and Design** – Your podcast's visual and sonic branding are crucial for attracting and retaining listeners. We'll explore how to create eye-catching artwork, choose music, and develop your podcast's unique style.

❖ **Chapter 6: Hosting and Publishing Your Podcast** – Discover how to choose a hosting platform, upload your episodes, and distribute your podcast to major directories like Apple Podcasts, Spotify, and Google Podcasts.

❖ **Chapter 7: Building and Engaging Your Audience** – Building a dedicated listener base is key to podcast success. We'll provide strategies for growing your audience, engaging with them, and turning them into loyal fans.

❖ **Chapter 8: Monetizing Your Podcast** – If you're interested in turning your podcast into a revenue stream, this chapter explores various monetization methods, including advertising, sponsorships, merchandise, and listener support.

❖ **Chapter 9: Podcast Promotion and Marketing** – Effective promotion is essential to ensure your podcast reaches a broader audience. Learn how to market your podcast through social media, email marketing, and other channels.

❖ **Chapter 10: Navigating Challenges and Pitfalls** – Every podcaster encounters challenges along the way. In this chapter, we'll address common issues and provide solutions to keep your podcast on track.

❖ **Chapter 11: The Future of Podcasting** – As the podcasting landscape evolves, we'll explore emerging trends and technologies, helping you stay ahead of the curve.

❖ **Chapter 12: Podcast Analytics and Performance Tracking** -Understanding how your podcast is performing is crucial for growth. In this chapter, we'll walk you through key metrics—like downloads, listener demographics, and engagement—that can help you fine-tune your content strategy and improve your overall podcast experience.

❖ **Chapter 13: Expanding Your Podcasting Network-** Once you've established your podcast, it's time to think about expansion. We'll cover how to grow beyond a single show through collaborations, starting a podcast network, and building partnerships within the podcasting community to further your reach.

## 1.3.2 How to Use This Book

THIS BOOK IS A VERSATILE resource that can be used in various ways, depending on your needs and preferences:

❖ **Sequential Reading**: If you're new to podcasting, consider reading the book from start to finish. This will provide you with a comprehensive understanding of the entire podcasting process, from conceptualization to promotion.

❖ **Topic-Specific Reference:** If you're already familiar with certain aspects of podcasting but need guidance on specific topics (e.g., recording techniques or audience engagement), you can jump directly to the relevant chapters.

❖ **Ongoing Reference:** Even after you've launched your podcast, this book can serve as a valuable reference. You can return to it whenever you encounter challenges, seek inspiration, or explore new avenues for podcast growth.

## 1.3.3 Your Podcasting Toolkit

TO EMBARK ON YOUR PODCASTING journey, you'll need a toolkit of essential resources and skills. Here's a preview of what's in your podcasting toolkit:

☑ **Recording Equipment:** Invest in a quality microphone, headphones, and audio interface to capture clear and professional-quality sound.

☑ **Recording and Editing Software:** Choose software such as Audacity, Adobe Audition, or GarageBand to record and edit your podcast episodes.

☑ **Hosting Platform:** Select a reliable podcast hosting platform like Libsyn, Podbean, or Spotify to store and distribute your podcast episodes.

☑ **Artwork and Branding:** Create eye-catching podcast artwork and establish your podcast's unique branding elements.

☑ **Online Presence:** Build a website or landing page for your podcast and establish a presence on social media platforms to connect with your audience.

☑ **Marketing and Promotion Tools:** Utilize email marketing, social media management tools, and promotional graphics to effectively market your podcast.

☑ **Analytics and Metrics:** Use podcast analytics platforms like Podtrac or Chartable to track listener metrics and gain insights into your audience's behavior.

☑ **Collaboration Tools:** If you plan to host interviews or collaborate with others, invest in tools like Zoom or Skype for remote recording.

## 1.3.4 Ready to Dive In?

BY REACHING THIS POINT in the book, you've taken the first steps toward becoming a podcaster. You're now equipped with a foundational understanding of podcasting, a roadmap for the chapters ahead, and the tools needed to start your journey. Whether your goal is to entertain, educate, inspire, or inform, podcasting offers a dynamic platform to share your voice with the world. So, are you ready to dive in? Let's explore the exciting world of podcast creation together.

# Chapter 2: Crafting Your Podcast Concept and Identifying Your Target Audience

Your podcast's concept is the heartbeat of your show, defining its unique identity and purpose. In this chapter, we'll explore the pivotal steps that set the stage for your podcasting journey, from defining your concept and identifying your audience to crafting a compelling Unique Selling Proposition (USP), structuring your episodes, and setting achievable goals.

# 2.1 Defining Your Podcast's Concept

At the core of your podcast lies its concept – the idea or theme that will captivate your audience. Defining your concept is the pivotal first step on your podcasting odyssey.

## 2.1.1 Brainstorming Your Podcast Concept

EXPLORING YOUR INTERESTS, passions, and expertise is the starting point for creating a compelling podcast. The process of brainstorming opens the door to creativity and innovation, allowing you to generate a list of potential podcast concepts.

### Explore Your Interests, Passions, and Expertise

To begin, reflect on your personal interests and areas of expertise. What topics excite you? What are you passionate about? Consider your hobbies, professional knowledge, and the subjects that genuinely captivate your attention. Your podcast concept should align with your interests to sustain your enthusiasm.

### Generate a List of Potential Podcast Concepts

Once you've identified areas of interest, start brainstorming ideas related to these topics. Don't censor yourself at this stage; aim for quantity over quality. The goal is to generate a diverse list of potential concepts that you can explore further.

## 2.1.2 Narrowing Down Your Options

HAVING GENERATED A list of potential podcast concepts, it's essential to evaluate and prioritize these ideas. Consider factors such as personal interest, audience appeal, and long-term sustainability when narrowing down your options.

⇨ **Evaluate and Prioritize Potential Concepts:** Begin by reviewing your list of potential concepts. Assess each idea based on its inherent appeal, feasibility, and potential to engage your target audience. Be open to refining or combining concepts to create a unique angle.

⇨ **Consider Personal Interest:** Your enthusiasm for the chosen concept is paramount. Ensure that the concept resonates with your interests and passions. A podcast concept aligned with your genuine curiosity and expertise is more likely to sustain your motivation over time.

⇨ **Audience Appeal:** While personal interest is crucial, also consider the concept's appeal to your intended audience. Does it address their interests or needs? Will it attract and retain listeners? Striking a balance between your passion and audience appeal is key.

⇨ **Sustainability:** Think long-term. Evaluate whether the chosen concept is sustainable because you can consistently create engaging content within that niche. Sustainability ensures the longevity of your podcast.

## 2.1.3 Crafting a Unique Angle

CREATING A DISTINCTIVE angle within your chosen concept is essential to set your podcast apart and offer something fresh and valuable to your audience.

### Create a Distinctive Angle Within Your Chosen Concept

While your chosen concept may not be unique, focus on developing a unique angle or perspective. Consider what sets your podcast apart from others in the same niche. What fresh insights, stories, or themes can you bring to the table?

### Ensure Your Podcast Offers Something Fresh and Valuable

Your podcast should provide value to your audience. Think about how your unique angle can contribute fresh perspectives, in-depth analysis, or unique experiences that listeners can't find elsewhere. Highlight what makes your podcast a must-listen in its niche.

## 2.1.4 Testing Your Podcast Concept

BEFORE FULLY COMMITTING to your podcast concept, it's essential to test it to ensure it aligns with your vision and resonates with your target audience.

⇨ **Create Pilot Episodes or Sample Content:** Consider producing pilot episodes or sample content to test your concept. These episodes serve as prototypes to gauge how well your concept works in practice. Use this stage to experiment with format, style, and content.

⇨ **Gauge Alignment with Your Vision:** Assess whether the produced content aligns with your original vision for the podcast. Does it capture the essence of your concept? Are you excited about the direction it's taking? Use this testing phase to make any necessary adjustments.

⇨ **Audience Resonance:** Seek feedback from a select group of listeners or potential audience members. Their input can provide valuable insights into how well your concept resonates with the target audience. Pay attention to their reactions and suggestions for improvement.

## 2.1.5 Aligning with Your Podcast Goals

TO ENSURE THE LONG-term success of your podcast, your concept must align with your overall podcasting goals.

**Ensure Your Concept Aligns with Overall Podcasting Goals**

Revisit your overarching podcasting goals. Whether your goal is to educate, entertain, inspire, or inform, your podcast concept should align with these objectives. Ensure that your concept serves the purpose you envision for your podcast.

**Connect Your Passion with the Purpose of Your Podcast**

Your passion for the chosen concept should seamlessly connect with the broader purpose of your podcast. This alignment ensures that your enthusiasm and dedication translate into meaningful content that resonates with your audience.

# 2.2 Identifying Your Target Audience

---

Your audience is the compass that guides your podcast's content and direction. Understanding your target audience is imperative for creating content that resonates deeply. In this section, we'll explore the crucial steps involved in identifying and connecting with your audience.

## 2.2.1 Creating Listener Personas

ONE OF THE MOST EFFECTIVE ways to understand and connect with your target audience is by creating listener personas. These detailed profiles represent your ideal audience members, offering insights into their demographics, interests, problems, and motivations.

### Demographics

Start by defining the basic demographic characteristics of your target audience. This includes age, gender, location, education level, and occupation. Understanding these demographic factors helps you tailor your content to their specific needs.

### Interests and Hobbies

Dive deeper into your audience's interests and hobbies. What are they passionate about? What do they enjoy doing in their free time? Identifying these interests allows you to create content that aligns with their leisure activities.

### Challenges and Pain Points

Listener personas should include information about the challenges and pain points your audience faces. What problems are they trying to solve, and what obstacles do they encounter? This insight enables you to address these issues in your podcast, providing valuable solutions and guidance.

### Motivations and Goals

Explore the motivations and goals of your target audience. What drives them? What are they looking to achieve in their personal or professional lives? Understanding their motivations helps you tailor your content to inspire and assist them on their journey.

## 2.2.2 Researching Your Audience

CONDUCT COMPREHENSIVE market research to gain a deeper understanding of your potential audience. Utilize surveys, social media polls, or engage in discussions within relevant online forums to gather valuable insights into their preferences, pain points, and the kind of content they genuinely enjoy.

In addition to creating listener personas, conducting thorough audience research is essential to gain a deeper understanding of your potential listeners. Here are key strategies for researching your audience:

★ **Surveys and Questionnaires:** Design and distribute surveys or questionnaires to your existing audience or target demographic. Ask questions about their preferences, interests, and challenges. Collecting this data provides valuable insights into their needs and desires.

★ **Social Media Engagement:** Engage with your audience on social media platforms. Participate in discussions, respond to comments, and conduct polls or Q&A sessions. Social media interactions offer a real-time glimpse into your audience's thoughts and preferences.

★ **Online Forums and Communities:** Join relevant online forums and communities where your target audience congregates. Participate in discussions, ask questions, and listen to their conversations. This allows you to tap into the collective wisdom and interests of your audience.

★ **Competitor Analysis:** Analyze other podcasts and content creators within your niche. Look at their audience demographics, engagement strategies, and content topics. Identify common themes and trends that resonate with your shared audience.

## 2.2.3 Identifying Pain Points

TO CREATE CONTENT THAT engages and serves your audience, pinpoint the problems or challenges they face within your chosen niche. Your podcast can provide solutions, insights, or entertainment related to these pain points, making it highly relevant and valuable. Identifying these pain points allows you to tailor your podcast to provide solutions, insights, or entertainment that directly address their needs.

### Conduct Problem-Solving Interviews

Consider conducting interviews or surveys specifically focused on identifying pain points within your niche. Engage with potential listeners or industry experts to gather firsthand information about the challenges your audience encounters.

### Analyze Existing Content

Review existing content within your niche, including podcasts, articles, and forums. Look for recurring questions, issues, or discussions that indicate common pain points. Your podcast can serve as a platform to provide clarity and solutions.

### Leverage Personal Experience

If applicable, draw from your personal experiences and challenges related to the niche. Sharing your journey and how you overcame obstacles can resonate strongly with your audience, as they may be facing similar difficulties.

## 2.2.4 Competitor Analysis

EXAMINE OTHER PODCASTS within your niche to discern their audience demographics and how they engage with their listeners. Identify gaps or areas where you can offer unique value or a fresh perspective.

Competitor analysis is a valuable tool for understanding your target audience. By examining other podcasts and content creators within your niche, you can discern audience demographics, engagement strategies, and content topics. Here's how to conduct effective competitor analysis:

✓ **Identify Key Competitors:** List the main competitors or podcasts in your niche. These are content creators who cater to a similar audience or address related topics.

✓ **Audience Demographics:** Study the audience demographics of your competitors. Look for patterns in age, gender, location, and other relevant factors. This information helps you refine your own target audience.

✓ **Content Themes and Topics:** Analyze the themes and topics covered by your competitors. What are the recurring themes in their content? Which topics generate the most engagement and interest among their audience?

✓ **Engagement Strategies:** Examine how your competitors engage with their listeners. Do they encourage audience participation through comments, questions, or social media? Identify successful engagement strategies that you can adapt to your podcast.

✓ **Content Gaps:** Identify gaps or areas where your competitors may not fully address their audience's needs. These gaps present opportunities for you to offer unique value or a fresh perspective.

In conclusion, identifying your target audience is a multifaceted process that involves creating listener personas, conducting audience research, pinpointing pain points, and analyzing competitors. These insights serve as the foundation for crafting content that resonates deeply with your audience, fostering strong connections, and ultimately, building a loyal listener base. Understanding your audience's demographics, interests, challenges, and motivations empowers you to create podcasts that are not only engaging but also genuinely impactful.

# 2.3 Crafting Your Unique Selling Proposition (USP)

———

Your Unique Selling Proposition (USP) is the beacon that attracts and retains your audience. It's the promise you make to your listeners, explaining why they should choose your podcast over others. In this section, we will delve into the intricacies of crafting a compelling USP:

## 2.3.1 Defining Your USP

BEFORE YOU CAN CRAFT an effective USP, you must first define it and understand what makes your podcast unique and appealing.

### Identifying Your Podcast's Unique Qualities

Your podcast's uniqueness lies in its distinct qualities that set it apart from others in your niche. Here's how to identify these unique qualities:

✓ **Content Differentiation:** Analyze the content you plan to offer. What topics, themes, or perspectives make your podcast stand out? Is there a fresh angle or innovative approach that you bring to the table? Identifying these unique content elements forms the foundation of your USP.

✓ **Your Expertise:** Consider your expertise or experiences that make you an authority in your chosen niche. Your expertise can be a powerful element of your USP, as it lends credibility and trustworthiness to your podcast.

✓ **Format and Style:** Assess the format and style of your podcast. Are you using a unique storytelling technique, interview style, or narrative approach? These elements contribute to the overall experience and can become part of your USP.

✓ **Originality:** Highlight any original features or segments that make your podcast truly unique. Whether it's a signature catchphrase, a recurring segment, or a particular style of humor, these distinctive elements can set your podcast apart.

**Aligning Your USP with Your Target Audience**

While identifying your podcast's unique qualities is essential, aligning them with your target audience's needs and preferences is equally crucial. Here's how to ensure alignment:

★ **Understanding Audience Needs:** Refer to the audience research you conducted earlier. What are the specific needs, interests, and pain points of your target audience? How can your podcast's unique qualities address and fulfill these needs?

★ **Tailoring Content:** Based on your understanding of audience needs, tailor your content and USP to cater directly to those requirements. Ensure that your podcast becomes a valuable resource for your audience by aligning its unique qualities with their expectations.

★ **Empathy and Relevance:** Approach your USP with empathy and a focus on relevance. Consider how your podcast can genuinely make a positive impact on your audience's lives. Addressing their specific pain points and providing solutions should be a core part of your USP.

## 2.3.2 Addressing Audience Needs

TO CRAFT AN EFFECTIVE USP, it's crucial to address the specific needs and challenges of your audience.

**Recognizing Audience Pain Points**

Identifying your audience's pain points is a critical step in addressing their needs effectively:

☑ **Empathetic Listening:** Listen empathetically to your target audience. Pay attention to their questions, concerns, and discussions related to your niche. What are the recurring challenges or problems they face? These pain points are opportunities for your podcast to provide solutions.

☑ **Feedback and Engagement:** Engage with your audience through social media, comments, and surveys. Encourage them to share their pain points and struggles. Analyze this feedback to identify common threads and prevalent issues.

☑ **Market Research:** Conduct thorough market research to gain insights into your audience's needs. Explore related forums, online communities, and discussions to identify the specific pain points within your niche.

## Tailoring Your USP to Solve Audience Challenges

Once you've identified audience pain points, tailor your USP to address and solve these challenges:

❖ **Solutions-Oriented USP:** Craft a USP that clearly conveys how your podcast provides solutions, insights, or support related to the specific challenges your audience faces. Your USP should highlight your podcast as a valuable resource for overcoming these obstacles.

❖ **Empowerment and Transformation:** Emphasize the transformation that your podcast can facilitate in the lives of your listeners. How will engaging with your content help them overcome obstacles, gain new perspectives, or improve their circumstances? This should be a core element of your USP.

❖ **Demonstrate Value:** Make it evident in your USP that your podcast offers tangible value. Whether it's actionable advice, in-depth analysis, or a source of inspiration, your USP should promise and deliver value consistently.

### 2.3.3 Articulating Your Unique Selling Proposition (USP)

YOUR UNIQUE SELLING Proposition (USP) is the compass that guides your podcast's identity and connects with your audience. In this section, we will delve into the crucial aspects of articulating your USP effectively:

**Crafting a Compelling USP Statement**

A compelling USP statement succinctly communicates the essence of your podcast's uniqueness and value proposition. It serves as the cornerstone of your podcast's identity:

☑ **Clarity and Conciseness:** A successful USP statement is crystal clear and concise. Avoid vague language or complex jargon that might confuse your audience. Your statement should be instantly understandable to anyone who encounters it.

☑ **Value Proposition:** Clearly state the value your podcast offers to listeners. What are the benefits of tuning in? How will their pain points be addressed, their questions answered, or their lives improved? Your USP should promise and deliver tangible value consistently.

☑ **Uniqueness:** Emphasize what sets your podcast apart from the competition. Highlight the elements that make it distinct within your niche. Whether it's your storytelling style, unique insights, or a novel approach to your subject matter, make it clear why your podcast is unlike any other.

☑ **Emotional Connection:** Consider how your USP can create an emotional connection with your audience. A compelling USP statement can evoke curiosity, inspiration, or a sense of belonging. Craft your USP with emotional resonance to deepen listener engagement and loyalty.

☑ **Consistency:** Ensure that your USP statement is consistent with the content and tone of your podcast. It should accurately represent what listeners can expect from your episodes. Consistency builds trust and helps listeners recognize your podcast's unique identity.

☑ **Relevance:** Your USP statement should resonate with your target audience's needs and interests. It should address the pain points you've identified and demonstrate how your podcast provides solutions, insights, or entertainment that aligns with their preferences.

Here's an example of a compelling USP statement: "Welcome to [Your Podcast Name], where we untangle the complexities of [Your Niche] with expert insights, captivating stories, and actionable advice. Join us as we journey together to explore, learn, and grow in the world of [Your Niche]."

**Integrating Your USP into Branding and Promotion**

Your USP should be seamlessly integrated into your podcast's branding and promotion strategies. Here's how to effectively incorporate your USP into your podcast's identity:

❖ **Consistency in Branding:** Ensure that your USP is consistently communicated across all aspects of your podcast's branding. This includes your website, podcast cover art, logo, social media profiles, and any merchandise. Consistency helps reinforce your unique identity.

❖ **Engagement:** Use your USP to engage with your audience. Encourage listeners to interact with your podcast by sharing their thoughts, questions, and experiences related to your unique aspects. Foster a sense of community around your USP, where listeners feel connected to your podcast's mission.

❖ **Promotional Messaging:** Infuse your USP into your promotional messaging. This includes crafting compelling podcast trailers, episode descriptions, and marketing campaigns that highlight the unique qualities and value your podcast offers. Your USP should be front and center in all promotional materials.

❖ **Storytelling:** Consider using storytelling techniques to convey your USP. Share anecdotes, case studies, or examples that illustrate how your podcast addresses audience needs and delivers on its promises. Stories are a powerful way to make your USP relatable and memorable.

❖ **Visual Elements:** Incorporate visual elements that reflect your USP into your branding. This could involve using specific colors, imagery, or design elements that resonate with your podcast's uniqueness. Visual consistency reinforces your USP visually.

❖ **Listener Testimonials:** Showcase listener testimonials that highlight how your podcast has fulfilled its USP. These authentic endorsements provide social proof of your podcast's value and uniqueness.

❖ **Live Up to Your USP:** Perhaps the most critical aspect of integrating your USP is to consistently deliver on your promises. Ensure that your podcast content aligns with your USP, providing listeners with the experience they expect based on your USP statement.

By crafting a compelling USP statement and integrating it into your branding and promotion efforts, you're effectively communicating your podcast's unique qualities and value proposition to your target audience. Your USP serves as the bridge that connects your podcast with listeners who are seeking precisely what you offer. It's a powerful tool for attracting and retaining your audience, ultimately leading to the success and impact of your podcast.

# 2.4 Structuring Your Episodes

———

Creating engaging and well-structured podcast episodes is vital for capturing your audience's attention and keeping them coming back for more. In this section, we will delve into the various aspects of structuring your episodes effectively to deliver valuable content.

## 2.4.1 Choosing an Episode Format

◈ **Narrative:** The narrative format involves storytelling, often with a beginning, middle, and end. It can be scripted or semi-scripted and is excellent for captivating storytelling and in-depth exploration of a topic.

◈ **Interview:** Interviews feature conversations with guests who bring expertise, insights, or unique perspectives to your podcast. This format adds variety and authority to your content.

◈ **Solo Commentary:** In solo commentary episodes, you share your thoughts, opinions, or expertise on a subject. It's an opportunity to connect with your audience personally.

◈ **Panel Discussion:** Panel discussions involve multiple hosts or experts discussing a topic. It's a dynamic format that offers diverse viewpoints and lively conversations.

◈ **Q&A or Listener Feedback:** Answering questions from your audience or addressing listener feedback fosters engagement and demonstrates a connection with your community.

◈ **Educational/Instructional:** Educational episodes provide valuable information or teach a specific skill. They are structured to deliver clear and actionable content.

⬦ **Roundup or Recap:** Roundup episodes summarize recent developments or events related to your niche. Recap episodes revisit key points from previous episodes, serving as a refresher.

⬦ **Storytelling and Personal Journals:** Storytelling episodes share personal anecdotes or experiences, connecting with listeners on a more emotional level.

⬦ **Hybrid Formats:** Hybrid formats combine elements from different formats to create unique episodes that suit your podcast's goals.

## 2.4.2 Planning Episode Content

❖ **Defining Episode Goals:** Clearly outline the objectives of each episode. What do you want your audience to gain or achieve after listening? Define the purpose and desired outcomes.

❖ **Creating an Outline or Script:** Develop a structured outline or script for your episode. Organize main points, subtopics, and transitions to ensure a coherent flow.

❖ **Incorporating Hooks and Teasers:** Engage your audience from the beginning with hooks or teasers. Pose intriguing questions, share compelling statistics, or use anecdotes to pique curiosity.

❖ **Balancing Content and Duration:** Strike a balance between providing valuable content and respecting your audience's time. Avoid unnecessary tangents and ensure that your episode aligns with its intended duration.

❖ **Segments and Transitions:** Divide your episode into segments to facilitate clarity and engagement. Use transitions to smoothly move between topics or segments.

❖ **Preparing Visual or Supplementary Materials:** If relevant, create visual aids, slides, or supplementary materials to enhance your content. Ensure that they complement the audio experience.

## 2.4.3 Engaging Introductions

### GRABBING ATTENTION

Start with a compelling opening that grabs your audience's attention. Consider using anecdotes, quotes, or intriguing facts to draw them in.

### Introducing the Episode Topic

Clearly introduce the main topic of your episode. Provide context to help listeners understand what to expect.

### Establishing Relevance

Explain why the episode's topic is relevant or important. Connect it to your audience's interests or needs.

### Teasing What's to Come

Give listeners a preview of what they can expect in the episode. Tease exciting segments, guest appearances, or key takeaways.

### Crafting Compelling Openers for Different Formats

Tailor your introduction to the specific format of the episode. For interviews, introduce your guest and highlight their expertise. For narratives, set the scene effectively.

## 2.4.4 Organizing Main Content

### CHRONOLOGICAL VS. TOPICAL Structure

Decide on the structure that best suits your content. A chronological structure follows a timeline, while a topical structure focuses on themes or subjects.

### Maintaining Flow and Cohesion

Ensure that your main content flows logically and cohesively. Use signposts, transitions, and summaries to guide listeners through the episode.

**Incorporating Examples and Case Studies**

Use real-world examples, case studies, or anecdotes to illustrate your points and make your content relatable.

**Involving Audience Interaction**

Encourage audience interaction throughout the episode. Pose questions, conduct polls, or invite feedback to keep listeners engaged.

**Handling Diverse Perspectives in Panel Discussions**

In panel discussions, manage diverse perspectives by moderating the conversation effectively. Ensure everyone has a chance to contribute and maintain a respectful atmosphere.

## 2.4.5 Enhancing Engagement

★ **Effective Use of Music and Sound Effects:** Enhance the listening experience by using music and sound effects strategically. Use them to create atmosphere or emphasize key points.

★ **Pacing and Timing Techniques:** Pay attention to pacing to maintain listener interest. Use timing techniques to build suspense, emphasize important information, or create emotional impact.

★ **Encouraging Audience Participation:** Encourage listeners to participate by asking questions, conducting polls, or inviting them to share their experiences.

★ **Incorporating Stories and Anecdotes:** Stories and personal anecdotes connect with listeners on a deeper level. Use them to illustrate concepts and make your content more relatable.

★ **Asking Thought-Provoking Questions:** Pose thought-provoking questions to stimulate critical thinking and engage your audience in meaningful discussions.

## 2.4.6 Calls to Action and Closing

⇨ **Summarizing Key Points:** Summarize the main takeaways or key points of the episode. Reinforce the value your audience has gained.

⇨ **Encouraging Listeners to Take Action:** Include clear calls to action (CTAs) that guide listeners on what to do next. Encourage subscriptions, reviews, website visits, or social media engagement.

⇨ **Promoting Subscription and Feedback:** Emphasize the benefits of subscribing to your podcast and leaving reviews. Also, invite listeners to provide feedback or suggest topics.

⇨ **Crafting Memorable Closers for Different Formats:** Tailor your closing for the episode format. In interviews, thank your guest and highlight their work. In narratives, leave listeners with a thought-provoking conclusion.

⇨ **Transitioning to Future Episodes:** Provide a teaser or hint about what listeners can expect in future episodes. Keep them excited and engaged.

## 2.4.7 Editing and Post-Production

☑ **Cleaning Audio and Removing Background Noise:** Ensure audio quality by removing background noise, echoes, or distractions during the editing process.

☑ **Enhancing Sound Quality:** Enhance sound quality using equalization, compression, and other audio processing techniques. Make sure voices are clear and balanced.

☑ **Adding Music and Effects:** Incorporate music, sound effects, or transitions during post-production to create a polished and engaging listening experience.

☑ **Removing Filler Words and Pauses:** Edit out filler words, long pauses, or any distracting elements that may hinder the flow of your episode.

☑ **Ensuring Consistency in Audio Levels:** Maintain consistent audio levels throughout the episode to prevent sudden volume changes that could disrupt the listener's experience.

## 2.4.8 Metadata and Episode Titles

☑ **Crafting Descriptive and Compelling Titles:** Create episode titles that are both descriptive and enticing. Titles should give listeners a clear idea of the episode's content while sparking interest.

☑ **Writing Engaging Episode Descriptions:** Craft engaging episode descriptions that provide additional context and encourage listeners to click and listen.

☑ **Optimizing Metadata for Search:** Include relevant keywords and phrases in your metadata to improve discoverability on podcast platforms. Make it easier for potential listeners to find your episodes.

☑ **Including Timestamps and Show Notes**: Consider adding timestamps and detailed show notes to your episodes. This helps listeners navigate content and find specific segments of interest.

## 2.4.9 Episode Length and Frequency

### DETERMINING IDEAL EPISODE Length

Assess your audience's preferences and your content's nature to determine the ideal episode length. Balance depth with brevity.

### Consistency in Release Schedule

Maintain a consistent release schedule to keep your audience engaged and aware of when to expect new episodes.

### Factors Influencing Episode Frequency

Consider factors like your production capacity, audience demand, and the complexity of your content when determining how often to release episodes.

### Adjusting Episode Length for Different Formats

Tailor the length of your episodes to the format. Narrative episodes may be longer, while educational episodes might benefit from a concise approach.

## 2.4.10 Listener Feedback and Adaptation

### GATHERING AND ANALYZING Listener Feedback

Actively seek and analyze listener feedback. Use surveys, social media polls, and direct communication to understand their preferences. .

### Using Feedback to Improve Structure

Utilize feedback to refine your episode structure, content, and style. Adapt to meet your audience's evolving needs and expectations.

### Adapting to Changing Audience Preferences

Be flexible in adapting your episode structure to changing audience preferences. Stay attuned to trends and shifts in your niche.

### Maintaining Flexibility in Episode Structure

While structure is essential, allow room for experimentation and adaptation to keep your podcast fresh and engaging.

By focusing on these aspects of structuring your episodes, you can create podcast content that resonates with your audience, keeps them engaged, and fosters a loyal listener community. Effective episode structuring contributes significantly to the success and impact of your podcast.

# 2.5 Setting Realistic Goals and Milestones

———

Podcasting is a journey filled with creativity, dedication, and growth. To navigate this journey successfully, you need a clear roadmap that sets you up for progress and achievement. In this chapter, we will explore the essential aspects of setting realistic goals and milestones for your podcasting adventure.

## 2.5.1 Defining Your Podcasting Objectives

### IDENTIFYING YOUR LONG-term Vision

Your podcast's journey begins with a vision, a long-term aspiration that encapsulates what you aim to achieve over time. Your long-term vision serves as the North Star that guides your podcasting efforts.

Whether it's becoming a recognized authority in your niche, reaching a specific number of loyal listeners, or making a meaningful impact on your audience, your long-term vision should be both inspiring and achievable.

### Clarifying your Podcast's Purpose

To set effective goals, you must have a crystal-clear understanding of your podcast's purpose. What do you want to convey to your audience? How do you want to make them feel? What value will you provide? Your podcast's purpose is the driving force behind your content, and it should align closely with your long-term vision.

### Aligning Goals with Your Passion

Passion fuels persistence. When setting goals for your podcast, ensure they resonate with your interests, expertise, and genuine enthusiasm. Aligning your goals with your passion increases your commitment to your podcasting journey, making the process more enjoyable and sustainable.

## 2.5.2 Establishing Achievable Milestones

### BREAKING LONG-TERM Goals into manageable steps

Long-term goals can be overwhelming if not broken down into smaller, manageable steps. Divide your long-term vision into achievable milestones. These milestones should represent significant progress points on your journey.

Consider milestones such as reaching a specific number of episodes, gaining a certain number of subscribers, or securing your first sponsor. Each milestone should be challenging yet attainable.

### Creating Short-term Objectives

To reach your milestones, you need short-term objectives that outline the specific tasks and actions required. Short-term objectives provide a clear roadmap for your podcasting efforts.

These objectives can encompass tasks like publishing regular episodes, conducting audience research, or improving your podcasting skills. Assign deadlines and timelines to each short-term objective to maintain focus and accountability.

## 2.5.3 Measuring Success and Key Performance Indicators (KPIs)

### IDENTIFYING METRICS for tracking progress

Success in podcasting is subjective and can vary from one podcaster to another. To measure your success effectively, identify the key performance indicators (KPIs) that matter most to you.

KPIs may include download numbers, listener engagement, website traffic, revenue generated, or social media interactions. Choose metrics that align with your goals and provide insights into your podcast's growth and impact.

### Defining Success in podcasting

Success is a personal journey, and it's crucial to define what it means to you. Whether success means achieving a specific number of downloads, earning a particular income, or gaining recognition in your niche, establish clear definitions of success that resonate with your podcast's purpose and your long-term vision.

### Using KPIs to evaluate performance

KPIs serve as benchmarks for evaluating your podcast's performance. Regularly track and analyze your chosen KPIs to assess progress toward your goals and milestones. Use these insights to make informed decisions and adjustments to your podcasting strategy.

## 2.5.4 Adapting and Revising Goals

### STAYING FLEXIBLE IN your podcasting journey

Flexibility is key to long-term success in podcasting. As you gain experience and gather feedback, you may need to adapt your goals and objectives to align with changing circumstances or audience preferences. Be open to adjustments and refinements in your podcasting journey.

### Adjusting Goals based on Feedback and Insights

Listener feedback and insights are valuable sources of information. Pay attention to audience preferences, suggestions, and trends within your niche. Use this feedback to fine-tune your goals and objectives, ensuring they remain relevant and impactful.

### Revising Objectives to reflect Changing Circumstances

The podcasting landscape evolves, and external factors can influence your journey. Be prepared to revise your objectives when necessary. Whether it's adapting to new technology, responding to shifts in your niche, or addressing unforeseen challenges, flexibility in goal setting allows you to navigate changes effectively.

## 2.5.5 Celebrating Milestones and Acknowledging

# Achievements

## RECOGNIZING AND REWARDING Progress

Milestones are significant achievements in your podcasting journey, and they deserve recognition. Celebrate your milestones, whether they involve reaching episode milestones, gaining a specific number of subscribers, or achieving personal podcasting goals.

Recognize your hard work and dedication, and don't hesitate to reward yourself for your achievements. Celebrating milestones motivates you to continue moving forward.

### Motivating Yourself through Milestones

Milestones provide motivation and serve as indicators of progress. When you reach a milestone, use it as fuel to keep your podcasting momentum strong. Reflect on how far you've come and set new goals to keep your passion and dedication alive.

### Building momentum for your ongoing podcasting journey

Momentum is a powerful force in podcasting. By celebrating milestones and acknowledging achievements, you maintain a positive and forward-moving attitude. This positivity fuels your ongoing podcasting journey, ensuring that you continue to grow, inspire, and make a meaningful impact on your audience.

In conclusion, setting realistic goals and milestones is a cornerstone of successful podcasting. It provides direction, motivation, and a framework for measuring progress. By defining objectives, establishing achievable milestones, measuring success with KPIs, staying adaptable, and celebrating achievements, you are well-equipped to navigate the dynamic world of podcasting effectively. Your goals and milestones are the compass that guides your journey, helping you turn your podcasting dreams into reality.

# Chapter 3: Creating Compelling Content

Creating compelling content is the essence of successful podcasting. This chapter delves into the crucial aspects of content creation, from research and content strategy to writing and production techniques, ensuring your podcast episodes captivate and engage your audience.

# 3.1 Research and Content Strategy

E ffective content creation begins with a solid research foundation and a well-thought-out strategy. In this section, we'll explore how to conduct research, define your podcast's niche, and craft a content strategy that aligns with your goals and audience.

## 3.1.1 The Power of Research

RESEARCH IS THE CORNERSTONE of compelling content. It not only informs your podcast episodes but also helps you understand your audience better. Here's how to harness the power of research:

**Audience Analysis**

Start by gaining a deep understanding of your target audience. Create listener personas, which are detailed profiles representing your ideal audience members. Consider demographics, interests, problems, motivations, and listening habits. Audience analysis informs your content decisions.

**Competitor Research**

Explore other podcasts in your niche. Identify what topics they cover, how they engage with their audience, and their strengths and weaknesses. Competitor research helps you find opportunities to differentiate your podcast and offer unique value.

**Keyword and Topic Research**

Use keyword research tools to identify popular topics and search terms related to your niche. This informs your content choices and can improve discoverability. Look for keywords with high search volume and relevance to your audience.

**Trends and Current Events**

Stay updated on industry trends and current events related to your podcast's subject matter. Timely content can attract a broader audience and demonstrate your expertise in real-time discussions.

**Guest Research**

If your podcast features guest interviews, research your guests thoroughly. Understand their background, expertise, and previous appearances. This ensures well-informed and engaging conversations.

## 3.1.2 Defining Your Niche

A WELL-DEFINED NICHE is essential for creating content that resonates with your audience. Here's how to identify and define your podcast's niche:

❖ **Passion and Expertise:** Consider your passions and areas of expertise. Choose a niche that aligns with your genuine interests, as your enthusiasm will shine through in your content. Podcasting is a long-term commitment, so pick a niche that sustains your motivation.

❖ **Audience Relevance:** While personal interest is crucial, also assess whether your chosen niche is relevant and appealing to your target audience. Balance your passion with audience appeal to ensure your podcast attracts and retains listeners.

❖ **Uniqueness and Angle:** Even within a niche, find a unique angle or perspective that sets your podcast apart. Consider what fresh insights, storytelling approaches, or themes you can bring to the table. Your podcast's distinctiveness is a key factor in attracting and retaining listeners.

## 3.1.3 Crafting Your Content Strategy

A CONTENT STRATEGY guides your podcast's direction and ensures consistency in your episodes. Here's how to craft an effective content strategy:

**Content Goals**

Define clear content goals aligned with your podcast's overall objectives. Are you aiming to educate, entertain, inspire, inform, or engage your audience? Your content goals guide episode creation.

**Episode Formats**

Determine the formats your podcast will follow. Common formats include interviews, storytelling, solo commentary, panel discussions, and Q&A sessions. Your chosen format should align with your content goals and audience preferences.

**Episode Frequency**

Decide on your podcast's release schedule. Will you publish episodes weekly, biweekly, monthly, or irregularly? Consistency is key to retaining and growing your audience.

**Episode Length**

Set guidelines for episode length. Consider your audience's preferences and the nature of your content. Some podcasts thrive with short, bite-sized episodes, while others delve deep with long-form content.

**Editorial Calendar**

Create an editorial calendar outlining upcoming episode topics, release dates, and any special episodes or series. A calendar helps you plan ahead and stay organized.

**Content Pillars**

Define content pillars or themes that guide your episode topics. These pillars ensure that your content remains focused and relevant to your niche.

**Audience Engagement**

Consider how you'll engage with your audience. Will you encourage listener feedback, host Q&A sessions, or involve your audience in content creation? Audience engagement fosters a sense of community.

**Monetization Strategy**

If you plan to monetize your podcast, outline your strategy. This could include advertising, sponsorships, listener support, or premium content.

By conducting thorough research, defining your podcast's niche, and crafting a content strategy, you lay the groundwork for creating compelling and relevant podcast episodes. These foundational steps ensure that your content aligns with your goals and resonates with your audience, setting the stage for a successful podcasting journey.

# 3.2 Developing Engaging Episode Formats

---

Choosing the right episode format is vital for delivering content that resonates with your audience. This section explores various episode formats, offering insights into how to select and implement them effectively.

## 3.2.1 Narrative Episodes

NARRATIVE EPISODES are storytelling at its finest. They take your audience on a journey, immersing them in compelling narratives, real-life experiences, or fictional tales. To create engaging narrative episodes:

**Engaging Storytelling**

Develop storytelling skills to captivate your audience. Craft narratives with clear beginnings, middles, and ends. Create relatable characters and build suspense to keep listeners hooked.

**Research and Preparation**

Extensive research is essential for narrative episodes. Whether you're sharing true stories or crafting fictional narratives, ensure your facts are accurate and your plots well-constructed.

**Sound Design**

Use sound effects, music, and ambient sounds to enhance the storytelling experience. These elements add depth and immersion to your narrative episodes.

**Character Development**

If your narrative involves characters, invest time in character development. Give them distinct personalities and motives to make the story more engaging.

**Consistency**

Maintain a consistent narrative style throughout your episodes. If you use a particular storytelling format or voice, stick to it to create a recognizable brand.

## 3.2.2 Interview Episodes

INTERVIEWS BRING FRESH perspectives and expert insights to your podcast. To conduct engaging interview episodes:

◈ **Guest Selection:** Choose guests who align with your podcast's niche and audience interests. Look for individuals with unique stories or expertise to share.

◈ **Preparation:** Thoroughly research your guests and their work. Prepare a list of questions but be flexible to allow for organic conversation.

◈ **Engaging Questions:** Craft questions that encourage insightful responses. Avoid yes/no questions and aim for open-ended queries that lead to meaningful discussions.

◈ **Active Listening:** During interviews, actively listen to your guests. Engage in the conversation, ask follow-up questions, and show genuine interest in their responses.

◈ **Editing**: Edit interview episodes for clarity and conciseness. Remove any tangents or irrelevant content to keep the episode engaging.

## 3.2.3 Solo Commentary Episodes

SOLO COMMENTARY EPISODES are an opportunity for you to share your thoughts, expertise, and insights directly with your audience. To create engaging solo commentary episodes, consider:

**Focused Topics**

Select specific topics or themes to explore in-depth. Avoid broad or vague subjects, as they can lead to disjointed episodes.

### Structure and Outline

Plan your episode's structure with a clear introduction, main points, and conclusion. Use an outline to stay organized during recording.

### Voice and Tone

Develop a consistent voice and tone for your solo episodes. This helps in building a connection with your audience over time.

### Engage Your Audience

Encourage audience interaction by posing questions, discussing listener feedback, or addressing comments and questions from previous episodes.

### Variety

While solo commentary is primarily about your perspective, incorporate diverse elements like anecdotes, examples, and personal experiences to keep episodes engaging.

## 3.2.4 Panel Discussion Episodes

PANEL DISCUSSIONS INVOLVE multiple participants offering diverse viewpoints on a particular topic. To host engaging panel discussion episodes:

### Diverse Panelists

Assemble a panel with diverse backgrounds, experiences, and perspectives related to the episode's topic.

### Moderation

Serve as a skilled moderator who guides the discussion, ensures everyone has a chance to speak, and keeps the conversation focused.

### Preparation

Provide panelists with the topic, questions, and discussion format in advance. This allows them to prepare and contribute meaningfully.

### Engage the Audience

Encourage listener participation by soliciting questions or topics from your audience. Include these in the discussion to foster a sense of community.

### Editing

Edit panel discussions for clarity and flow. Remove any tangential or repetitive content to maintain engagement.

## 3.2.5 Q&A or Listener Feedback Episodes

Q&A OR LISTENER FEEDBACK episodes involve addressing questions, comments, or feedback from your audience. To create engaging Q&A episodes:

### Audience Engagement

Encourage listeners to submit their questions or feedback through various channels, such as email, social media, or a dedicated podcast voicemail.

### Organization

Categorize and prioritize the questions or comments you receive. This helps in structuring the episode effectively.

### Variety and Depth

Mix shorter, straightforward answers with more in-depth discussions of selected questions. This keeps the episode dynamic and informative.

### Acknowledgment

Recognize and appreciate listener contributions by mentioning their names or social media handles. This encourages ongoing engagement.

### Timeliness

Address recent or relevant questions and feedback to demonstrate that you value your audience's input.

Choosing the right episode format and implementing it effectively is key to delivering engaging content. Whether you opt for narrative, interview, solo commentary, panel discussion, or Q&A episodes, consider your podcast's niche, audience preferences, and content goals. By tailoring your format to your unique podcast, you'll create episodes that captivate and retain your listeners.

# 3.3 Scriptwriting and Storytelling Techniques

---

I n the realm of podcasting, scriptwriting and storytelling are fundamental skills for creating captivating and engaging audio content. This chapter delves into the essential techniques and strategies that will empower you to craft compelling podcast scripts and deliver stories that resonate with your audience.

## 3.3.1 Understanding Your Podcasting Audience

BEFORE YOU EMBARK ON crafting your podcast script, it's imperative to gain a deep understanding of your audience:

**Audience Demographics:** Start by defining the demographic characteristics of your target audience. Consider factors such as age, gender, location, and interests. These insights will help you tailor your content to match your listeners' profile.

**Listener Surveys:** Actively engage with your audience through surveys and feedback mechanisms. Learn about their preferred topics, desired episode lengths, and favored podcasting styles. This valuable information will shape your content strategy.

**In-Depth Research:** Dive into comprehensive research to uncover your audience's pain points, interests, and challenges within your niche. Your podcast should provide solutions, insights, or entertainment relevant to these areas.

## 3.3.2 Crafting Engaging Openings

THE INITIAL MOMENTS of your podcast episode are pivotal in capturing your audience's attention. Employ the following techniques to craft compelling introductions:

⇨ **Hook Your Audience:** Start with an attention-grabbing hook or pose a thought-provoking question that arouses curiosity and compels listeners to continue.

⇨ **Introduction to the Topic:** Clearly articulate the central theme of the episode and explain its significance. Convey why it matters and why listeners should invest their time in listening further.

⇨ **Building a Connection:** Forge a personal connection with your audience by sharing relatable stories, personal anecdotes, or relevant experiences. This establishes empathy and a sense of rapport.

## 3.3.3 Developing Engaging Podcast Content

ONCE YOU HAVE CAPTURED your audience's attention, it's crucial to focus on developing content that sustains their engagement:

**Clarity and Structural Organization**

Maintain a clear and well-structured narrative throughout your podcast script. Use headings, bullet points, or timestamps to guide your storyline.

**Harnessing Storytelling Elements**

Even in non-narrative episodes, integrate storytelling elements such as character development, conflict, and resolution. Storytelling adds depth and resonance to your content.

**Vivid Language**

Utilize descriptive language that paints a vivid mental picture for your listeners. Engage their senses with vivid and evocative descriptions.

**Analogies and Metaphors**

Simplify complex ideas by employing analogies or metaphors that make them relatable and comprehensible.

### 3.3.4 Writing for the Ear

PODCAST SCRIPTS ARE unique in that they are meant to be heard, not just read. Consider the following auditory factors:

**Conversational Tone**

Write in a conversational and relatable tone. Utilize contractions and address your audience directly, creating the impression of an intimate one-on-one conversation.

**Concise Sentences**

Keep your sentences succinct and to the point. Lengthy and convoluted sentences can be challenging for listeners to follow in an audio format.

**Pacing and Emphasis**

Use punctuation to indicate pauses or emphasize particular points. Commas signal brief pauses, while ellipses (...) denote longer ones.

**Tonal Variation**

Reflect the appropriate tone for your content. If your episode is informative, maintain a neutral tone. However, for storytelling episodes, infuse your narration with the appropriate emotions and enthusiasm.

### 3.3.5 Audience Engagement

SUSTAINING AUDIENCE engagement throughout your podcast episode is vital:

◈ **Questions and Prompts:** Include thought-provoking questions or prompts that encourage listener reflection or participation.

◈ **Calls to Action:** Integrate clear calls to action (CTAs) that prompt specific responses from your audience. These actions can range from subscribing and leaving reviews to sharing your podcast with others.

◈ **Incorporate Listener Feedback:** Acknowledge listener comments or questions related to previous episodes. Demonstrating that you value their input can foster a sense of community and connection.

◈ **Humor and Anecdotes:** Use humor and personal anecdotes judiciously to keep the episode engaging and relatable, resonating with your audience.

## 3.3.6 Editing and Polishing Your Podcast Script

AFTER COMPLETING THE initial draft of your script, the editing phase is crucial:

☑ **Proofreading:** Carefully proofread your script to eliminate grammar, spelling, and punctuation errors. A polished script enhances your podcast's credibility.

☑ **Read-Aloud Checks:** Conduct read-aloud checks to ensure that your script flows naturally and sounds engaging when spoken aloud.

☑ **Length Considerations:** Review your script's length to ensure it aligns with your target episode duration.

☑ **Sensitivity Review:** If your podcast addresses sensitive topics, consider conducting a sensitivity review to prevent inadvertently offending or alienating your audience.

## 3.3.7 Structuring Your Podcast's Story Arc and Episode Progression

FOR SERIALIZED OR NARRATIVE shows, it's vital to consider the overall story arc and episode progression:

**Plot Development**

Plan how each episode contributes to the overarching narrative or theme of your podcast. Ensure that each episode advances the story or discussion in a meaningful way.

### Episode Progression

Maintain a logical progression from one episode to the next. Each episode should build upon the previous one, either by offering new insights or by advancing the storyline.

### Hooks and Cliffhangers

Strategically place hooks or cliffhangers at the end of episodes to entice listeners to return for subsequent episodes. These elements can create anticipation and suspense.

## 3.3.8 Collaborative Scriptwriting

IF YOU COLLABORATE with others on your podcast, maintaining consistency and clarity is paramount:

### Style Guide

Develop a comprehensive style guide that outlines writing conventions, tone, and formatting rules. This guide ensures uniformity in your podcast scripts.

### Version Control

Implement version control tools to track script revisions and edits, especially when collaborating with remote team members or co-hosts.

### Read-Aloud Collaborative Checks

Have team members read scripts aloud to ensure they sound cohesive and maintain a consistent tone and style.

Effective scriptwriting and storytelling are fundamental skills that will enable you to create memorable and engaging podcast episodes. Whether you are crafting narrative storytelling, interview-based discussions, or solo commentary, these techniques will help you connect with your audience, leaving them eager for more. Podcasting is a medium of storytelling and connection, and mastering these skills will elevate your content and deepen your audience's engagement.

# 3.4 Finding and Booking Guests

———

Podcasts thrive on engaging and diverse content, making guest appearances a valuable asset for creators. In this chapter, we delve into the art of finding, approaching, and booking guests for your podcast. Whether you're seeking experts, thought leaders, or fascinating individuals, these strategies will help you bring fresh perspectives to your show.

## 3.4.1 Defining Your Guest Criteria

BEFORE EMBARKING ON your guest search, clarify your criteria to ensure the right fit:

★ **Relevance:** Determine how closely potential guests align with your podcast's theme, topics, or niche. Relevance ensures that their insights resonate with your audience.

★ **Expertise:** Identify the level of expertise or unique perspective your guest should possess. Consider whether they should be specialists in their field, possess a particular experience, or bring a fresh angle to your discussions.

★ **Audience Appeal:** Evaluate the potential guest's appeal to your audience. Will their presence attract and engage your listeners? Assess factors such as their reputation, following, and appeal.

★ **Diversity:** Consider diversity in its various forms, such as gender, race, background, and expertise. Diverse guests can offer a broader range of perspectives and enrich your podcast's content.

## 3.4.2 Guest Sourcing Strategies

EXPLORE VARIOUS STRATEGIES for finding suitable podcast guests:

☐ **Personal Network:** Tap into your personal and professional network to identify potential guests. Contacts from your industry, colleagues, friends, or acquaintances may have valuable connections.

☐ **Guest Pitches:** Create a submission form or email address on your podcast website, allowing potential guests to pitch themselves. Encourage them to share their expertise and why they'd be an excellent fit for your show.

☐ **Guest Booking Services:** Utilize guest booking services or agencies that specialize in connecting podcasters with suitable guests. These services streamline the guest-finding process.

☐ **Social Media:** Engage on social media platforms to identify potential guests who actively participate in discussions related to your podcast's niche. Direct messages or mentions can initiate contact.

☐ **Podcast Guest Directories:** Explore podcast guest directories and databases that catalog individuals interested in guest appearances. These platforms categorize guests by expertise and availability.

## 3.4.3 The Guest Outreach Process

ONCE YOU'VE IDENTIFIED potential guests, the outreach process is crucial to secure their participation:

### Crafting Invitations

Create personalized and compelling invitations that clearly convey the benefits of appearing on your podcast. Highlight why their insights are valuable to your audience.

### Email Communication

Send well-crafted emails introducing yourself, your podcast, and your invitation. Clearly outline the logistics, such as recording dates, platforms, and episode expectations.

**Follow-Up**

Send polite follow-up emails if you don't receive a response within a reasonable time frame. Persistence can often lead to positive outcomes.

**Leverage Your Network**

If you share mutual connections, mention them in your outreach. Common connections can establish trust and credibility.

**Professionalism**

Maintain professionalism throughout your communication. Respect potential guests' time and preferences and be flexible in scheduling.

## 3.4.4 Preparing for Guest Interviews

EFFECTIVE PREPARATION is key to successful guest interviews:

**Research**

Thoroughly research your guest, their background, achievements, and previous interviews. Understanding their perspective enhances the quality of your questions.

◇ **Interview Format:** Determine the interview format that best suits your podcast and guest. Options include solo interviews, panel discussions, debates, or co-hosted conversations.

◇ **Questions:** Prepare a list of questions that align with your episode's theme and objectives. Develop open-ended questions that encourage in-depth responses and storytelling.

◇ **Logistics:** Communicate logistical details clearly, including recording platforms, time zones, and technical requirements. Ensure your guest has all the necessary information to join the recording seamlessly.

## 3.4.5 Conducting Engaging Guest Interviews

DURING THE INTERVIEW, focus on creating an engaging and insightful conversation:

### Active Listening

Actively listen to your guest's responses and adapt your follow-up questions based on their insights. Show genuine interest in their perspectives.

### Conversation Flow

Maintain a natural flow of conversation rather than adhering strictly to your prepared questions. Allow for spontaneous and engaging discussions.

### Respect and Inclusivity

Foster an inclusive and respectful environment. Encourage diverse perspectives and ensure that all voices are heard and valued.

### Timing

Keep an eye on the interview's timing to ensure it aligns with your episode length. Guide the conversation to cover essential points within the allotted time.

## 3.4.6 Post-Interview Actions

AFTER THE INTERVIEW, there are essential steps to follow:

★ **Thank You:** Express gratitude to your guest for their time and insights. A simple thank-you email, or message can leave a positive impression.

★ **Editing and Production:** Edit the interview to enhance audio quality, remove distractions, and ensure clarity. Incorporate the interview seamlessly into your podcast episode.

★ **Promotion:** Share information about the upcoming episode with your guest, including its release date and promotional plans. Encourage your guest to share the episode with their audience, increasing its reach.

★ **Feedback and Testimonials:** After the episode is published, seek feedback and testimonials from your guest. Their positive comments can serve as social proof and enhance your podcast's credibility.

★ **Maintaining Relationships:** Keep in touch with your previous guests. Building and nurturing relationships can lead to return appearances or collaborations in the future.

## 3.4.7 Handling Rejections and Challenges

NOT ALL OUTREACH ATTEMPTS will result in guest bookings. It's essential to handle rejections and challenges gracefully:

**Rejections**

Accept rejections graciously and professionally. Thank the potential guest for considering your invitation, and keep the door open for future opportunities.

**Challenges**

Be prepared to navigate challenges such as scheduling conflicts, technical issues, or unexpected cancellations. Flexibility and problem-solving skills are valuable in overcoming these obstacles.

## 3.4.8 Legal and Ethical Considerations

CONSIDER LEGAL AND ethical aspects related to guest appearances:

**Release Forms**

Depending on your jurisdiction, it may be necessary to obtain release forms or consent agreements from your guests, granting permission to use their likeness, voice, or content.

**Intellectual Property**

Respect intellectual property rights. Ensure that your guests have the necessary permissions to share copyrighted material during the interview.

**Transparency**

Maintain transparency with your guests regarding the episode's content, context, and potential impact. Seek their approval for any significant edits or changes.

## 3.4.9 Ongoing Guest Management

AS YOUR PODCAST GROWS, managing guest appearances becomes an ongoing process:

**Guest Calendar**

Maintain a guest calendar to track upcoming appearances, recording dates, and episode release schedules. This helps in effective planning and organization.

**Guest Diversity**

Continuously seek diverse voices and perspectives to enrich your podcast's content. Expanding your network and reaching out to a broad range of potential guests can contribute to a more inclusive podcast.

**Audience Feedback**

Encourage your audience to provide feedback on guest appearances. Their input can help you identify strengths and areas for improvement in your guest selection process.

By mastering the art of finding and booking guests for your podcast, you open doors to a world of enriching conversations and valuable insights. Each guest brings a unique perspective, contributing to the growth and appeal of your podcast. With careful planning, professionalism, and an inclusive approach, your podcast can become a platform for diverse voices and engaging content.

# 3.5: Copyright and Legal Considerations for Podcasts

---

Podcast creators must navigate a complex legal landscape to ensure their content remains compliant with copyright and other legal regulations. Understanding these considerations is crucial for both protecting your podcast and respecting the rights of others. In this chapter, we delve into various legal aspects that every podcaster should be aware of.

## 3.5.1 Copyright Basics

COPYRIGHT LAWS GRANT creators exclusive rights to their original works. For podcasters, this means respecting copyright when using music, literature, art, and other protected content. Here's an overview:

**Copyright Ownership**

Understand that the creator or rights holder owns the copyright to their work automatically upon creation. Registration is not required, though it offers additional legal benefits.

**Fair Use Doctrine**

Familiarize yourself with the "fair use" doctrine, a legal principle allowing limited use of copyrighted material without permission for purposes such as commentary, criticism, news reporting, or education. However, the scope of fair use can be subjective and should be assessed carefully.

**Public Domain**

Content in the public domain is free to use without copyright restrictions. Be cautious when assuming a work is in the public domain, as it depends on factors like the work's age and origin.

## 3.5.2 Music Licensing and Usage

MUSIC CAN SIGNIFICANTLY enhance a podcast's appeal, but it's a copyright minefield. To avoid legal issues, consider these aspects:

❖ **Licensed Music:** Use music that you have the appropriate licenses for. Stock music libraries, royalty-free tracks, and licensed music platforms provide options for legal music use in podcasts.

❖ **Podsafe Music:** Explore podsafe music, which artists and labels explicitly permit for podcast use without extensive licensing. Many indie musicians offer their music as podsafe, often under Creative Commons licenses.

❖ **Royalty-Free Music:** Royalty-free music can be used in podcasts for a one-time fee, without recurring royalties. Ensure you understand the licensing terms and restrictions.

❖ **Attribution:** When using music under certain licenses, you may need to provide attribution to the composer or source. Always follow attribution requirements to comply with licensing terms.

## 3.5.3 Content Permissions and Releases

USING CONTENT CREATED by others, including interviews, guest appearances, or third-party materials, requires proper permissions and releases:

### Guest Releases

Obtain written releases from podcast guests, granting permission to use their voice, likeness, and any provided materials. This helps protect against legal disputes in the future.

### Third-Party Materials

If you include third-party materials (e.g., sound effects, clips, or excerpts) in your podcast, ensure you have the necessary rights or licenses to use them.

**Public Domain and Creative Commons**

Utilize public domain or Creative Commons content when appropriate, ensuring adherence to the specific license terms (e.g., attribution or non-commercial use).

## 3.5.4 Privacy and Defamation Concerns

PRIVACY AND DEFAMATION issues can arise when discussing individuals or entities on your podcast:

**Privacy Laws**

Familiarize yourself with privacy laws in your jurisdiction, as they vary widely. Respect individuals' rights by obtaining consent for personal information sharing.

**Defamation**

Avoid making false statements that harm someone's reputation. Verify facts and exercise caution when discussing sensitive topics.

## 3.5.5 Advertising and Sponsorship Agreements

MONETIZING YOUR PODCAST often involves advertising and sponsorship agreements:

**Advertising Content**

Clearly disclose to your audience when content is sponsored or includes advertising. Maintain transparency to build trust with your listeners.

**Sponsorship Agreements**

Ensure that your sponsorship agreements align with your podcast's values and content. Review terms and conditions carefully to avoid conflicts.

## 3.5.6 Trademarks and Branding

PROTECT YOUR PODCAST'S brand and intellectual property:

**Trademark Registration**

Consider trademark registration for your podcast's name, logo, or branding elements. This helps safeguard your identity and prevent others from using similar branding.

**Respect Others' Trademarks**

Avoid infringing on others' trademarks, as it can lead to legal disputes. Conduct searches to ensure your branding doesn't conflict with existing trademarks.

## 3.5.7 International Considerations

PODCASTS HAVE A GLOBAL reach, so it's essential to understand international copyright and legal implications:

**International Copyright Treaties**

Many countries are signatories to international copyright treaties. Familiarize yourself with these treaties to navigate cross-border copyright issues.

**Jurisdictional Variations**

Legal regulations, including copyright and defamation laws, can differ significantly between countries. Consider the potential impact of international listenership on your podcast's content and legal compliance.

## 3.5.8 Legal Consultation

WHEN IN DOUBT, SEEK legal counsel:

**Legal Advice**

If you have concerns about specific legal aspects of your podcast, consult with an attorney experienced in intellectual property and media law. Legal advice can provide clarity and help you make informed decisions.

Navigating the legal landscape of podcasting is essential for protecting your podcast and its creators. By understanding copyright basics, respecting licensing and permissions, being mindful of privacy and defamation concerns, and staying informed about international considerations, you can create and share content with confidence while minimizing legal risks.

# Chapter 4: Recording and Production

# 4.1 Choosing the Right Equipment

═══

Selecting the appropriate podcasting equipment is a critical decision that impacts the audio quality and overall production value of your show. In this chapter, we explore various equipment options and considerations to help you make informed choices.

## 4.1.1 Microphones

MICROPHONES ARE AT the core of podcasting equipment. Choosing the right microphone for your needs is essential for capturing high-quality audio. Consider the following aspects:

**Dynamic vs. Condenser Microphones**

Dynamic microphones are durable and less sensitive to background noise, making them suitable for various recording environments. Condenser microphones offer superior audio quality and sensitivity, ideal for controlled studio settings.

**USB vs. XLR Microphones**

USB microphones connect directly to your computer and are convenient for beginners or those on a budget. XLR microphones provide more versatility and superior sound quality but require an audio interface or mixer.

**Polar Patterns**

Different microphones have varying polar patterns (e.g., cardioid, omnidirectional, bidirectional). Choose a polar pattern that suits your recording environment and reduces unwanted noise.

**Budget Considerations**

Microphone prices range from budget-friendly to professional-grade. Determine your budget and balance it with your desired audio quality.

## 4.1.2 Headphones

QUALITY HEADPHONES are essential for monitoring audio during recording and editing. Consider the following factors when selecting headphones:

**Closed-Back vs. Open-Back**

Closed-back headphones provide sound isolation, reducing bleed into the microphone. Open-back headphones offer a more natural sound but may not be suitable for noisy environments.

**Over-Ear vs. On-Ear**

Over-ear headphones encircle the ears, providing comfort and better noise isolation. On-ear headphones rest directly on the ears and are more compact but may be less comfortable during extended use.

**Frequency Response**

Look for headphones with a balanced frequency response to ensure accurate audio monitoring.

**Comfort and Fit**

Choose comfortable headphones that you can wear for extended periods without discomfort.

## 4.1.3 Audio Interfaces and Mixers

AUDIO INTERFACES AND mixers are essential for connecting microphones and headphones to your computer and controlling audio levels. Consider these factors:

**Number of Inputs:** Determine how many microphones you'll be using and choose an interface or mixer with the corresponding number of inputs.

**Preamps:** Quality preamps are crucial for clean and clear audio. Consider interfaces or mixers with high-quality preamps for professional results.

**Connectivity:** Ensure compatibility with your microphones (XLR or USB) and computer (USB, Thunderbolt, or other connections).

**Control Features:** Some mixers offer advanced features like equalization, compression, and effects. Consider your audio processing needs.

## 4.1.4 Acoustic Treatment

CREATING AN ACOUSTICALLY treated recording space is essential for minimizing unwanted reflections and background noise. Consider these elements:

### Soundproofing

Reduce external noise by soundproofing your recording space with materials like acoustic panels, bass traps, and soundproof curtains.

### Acoustic Panels

Install acoustic panels on walls and ceilings to control reverberation and echo. These panels come in various sizes and designs.

### Diffusers

Diffusers scatter sound waves, improving the overall sound quality of your space. Consider diffusers for a well-rounded acoustic treatment.

### Isolation Shields

Isolation shields or reflection filters can help reduce room reflections and isolate the microphone.

## 4.1.5 Recording Software

CHOOSING THE RIGHT recording software, also known as a digital audio workstation (DAW), is crucial for efficient podcast production. Consider these factors:

☑ **Ease of Use:** Select a DAW that aligns with your skill level. Many DAWs offer both basic and advanced features.

☑ **Compatibility:** Ensure compatibility with your operating system (e.g., Windows, macOS) and hardware.

☑ **Audio Editing Features**: Look for essential editing tools such as cutting, copying, pasting, and adding effects.

☑ **Multitrack Recording:** For podcasts with multiple hosts or guests, choose a DAW that supports multitrack recording for individual audio tracks.

## 4.1.6 Accessories and Extras

SEVERAL ACCESSORIES and extras can enhance your podcasting setup:

**Microphone Stands**

Sturdy microphone stands prevent vibrations and ensure microphone stability during recording.

**Pop Filters**

Pop filters reduce plosive sounds (e.g., "p" and "b" sounds) and protect microphones from saliva.

**Shock Mounts**

Shock mounts isolate microphones from vibrations and handling noise.

**Cables**

High-quality XLR or USB cables are essential for reliable connections.

**Boom Arms**

Boom arms provide flexibility in microphone positioning and help declutter your workspace.

**Portable Recorders**

Consider portable recorders for on-the-go podcasting or recording interviews outside the studio.

Choosing the right podcasting equipment involves evaluating your specific needs, budget, and recording environment. Whether you're a beginner or a seasoned podcaster, making informed equipment choices is essential for producing professional-quality podcasts.

# 4.2: Setting Up Your Recording Space

---

Creating an optimal recording environment is vital for producing high-quality podcast content. In this chapter, we delve into the considerations and steps for setting up your recording space, whether it's a dedicated studio or a makeshift area.

## 4.2.1 Space Selection

SELECTING THE RIGHT location for your recording space is the first crucial step. Consider the following factors:

⇨ **Room Choice:** Choose a room with minimal external noise, such as traffic or neighbors. Ideally, select a space with limited ambient sounds like air conditioning or refrigerator noise.

⇨ **Size and Layout:** The size of the room matters. Smaller rooms tend to have more noticeable sound reflections. Consider the layout to accommodate your recording equipment and seating arrangements.

⇨ **Accessibility:** Ensure easy access to power outlets and internet connections. Accessibility will affect your equipment setup and recording comfort.

## 4.2.2 Acoustic Treatment

ACOUSTIC TREATMENT is essential for controlling sound reflections and ensuring clean audio recordings:

### Soundproofing

Implement soundproofing techniques to minimize noise from outside the recording space. This may involve sealing gaps, adding weather stripping to doors, or installing double-glazed windows.

**Acoustic Panels**

Mount acoustic panels on the walls and ceiling to absorb sound reflections and prevent echo. These panels come in various sizes and designs, allowing you to customize your space.

**Bass Traps**

Use bass traps in corners to address low-frequency sound issues and reduce bass buildup.

**Diffusers**

Diffusers scatter sound waves, creating a more balanced acoustic environment. They're especially useful in larger rooms.

**Isolation Shield**

Consider using an isolation shield or reflection filter around your microphone to minimize room reflections and focus on your voice.

## 4.2.3 Room Preparation

PREPARE YOUR RECORDING space for optimal audio quality:

☑ **Declutter:** Remove unnecessary items and clutter from the room to reduce sound reflections and echoes. An uncluttered space also provides better ventilation and comfort during recording.

☑ **Furniture:** Furnish the room with appropriate seating and tables for hosts and guests. Consider furniture with acoustic properties if possible.

☑ **Lighting:** Ensure adequate lighting for your recording space. Soft, diffused lighting is preferable to harsh, direct lighting, which can create glare and discomfort.

☑ **Ventilation:** Maintain good airflow and ventilation to prevent overheating and discomfort during recording sessions. Avoid noisy fans or air conditioning units that could interfere with audio.

## 4.2.4 Equipment Placement

PROPER PLACEMENT OF your recording equipment is essential for achieving the best audio results:

◇ **Microphone Positioning:** Position your microphone correctly to capture your voice while minimizing background noise. Use a sturdy microphone stand or boom arm to avoid vibrations.

◇ **Headphones:** Place headphone jacks and audio interfaces within easy reach to make real-time monitoring and adjustments convenient.

◇ **Computer Setup:** Set up your computer or recording device on a stable surface within arm's reach. Ensure it's configured with the necessary recording software and plugins.

## 4.2.5 Soundproofing and Noise Reduction

MINIMIZING EXTERNAL and internal noise is crucial for achieving pristine audio quality:

### Seal Windows and Doors

Use weather stripping to seal gaps around windows and doors to reduce external noise infiltration.

### Rugs and Curtains

Lay rugs on hard floors and hang thick curtains to absorb sound reflections and reduce echo.

### Background Noise

Turn off or mute noisy appliances like fans, air conditioners, and refrigerators during recording.

**Noise Isolation**

If external noise remains a concern, consider investing in noise isolation solutions like acoustic barriers or double-glazing windows.

## 4.2.6 Cable Management

KEEP CABLES ORGANIZED to prevent tripping hazards and maintain a neat recording space:

**Cable Ties:** Use cable ties or Velcro straps to bundle and secure cables, preventing tangling and accidents.

**Cable Channels:** Install cable channels or raceways along walls or baseboards to conceal and protect cables.

**Labeling:** Label your cables to easily identify connections and prevent confusion.

Creating an effective recording space involves attention to detail and a commitment to optimizing audio quality. Whether you have a dedicated studio or a makeshift setup, implementing acoustic treatment, organizing equipment, and reducing background noise will significantly enhance your podcast recordings.

# 4.3: Recording Techniques and Best Practices

———

Recording your podcast is where the magic happens. This chapter explores the fundamental recording techniques and best practices that will help you capture high-quality audio and ensure a smooth recording process.

## 4.3.1 Microphone Selection

SELECTING THE RIGHT microphone is a critical decision in achieving excellent audio quality:

### Dynamic vs. Condenser

Dynamic microphones are durable and handle high sound pressure levels well, making them suitable for various environments. Condenser microphones are more sensitive and capture a broader frequency range, ideal for studio setups.

### USB vs. XLR

USB microphones are user-friendly and plug directly into your computer. XLR microphones offer superior audio quality and are commonly used in professional setups.

### Polar Patterns

Consider the microphone's polar pattern (e.g., cardioid, omnidirectional, or bidirectional) based on your recording environment and the number of hosts or guests.

## 4.3.2 Microphone Placement

PROPER MICROPHONE PLACEMENT is essential for capturing clear and balanced audio:

### Distance and Angle

Position the microphone approximately 6 to 12 inches from your mouth, slightly off-center to reduce plosives (popped "P" sounds) and sibilance (hissing "S" sounds).

### Pop Filter

Use a pop filter or windscreen to further reduce plosives and breath noise. Place it between your mouth and the microphone.

### Shock Mount

If possible, use a shock mount to isolate the microphone from vibrations and handling noise.

## 4.3.3 Recording Environment

CREATING AN ACOUSTICALLY controlled recording environment is crucial for clean audio:

### Quiet Space

Choose a quiet room with minimal background noise. Consider soundproofing and acoustic treatment to reduce echo and reflections.

### Closed Doors and Windows

Ensure doors and windows are closed to minimize external noise infiltration.

### Curtains and Carpets

Use curtains, carpets, or acoustic panels to absorb sound and reduce reflections.

**Background Noise:** Turn off or mute any appliances or fans that could introduce unwanted noise.

## 4.3.4 Monitoring and Headphones

USING HEADPHONES FOR real-time monitoring is essential for assessing audio quality:

**Closed-Back Headphones:** Choose closed-back headphones to prevent sound leakage into the microphone.

**Volume Control:** Keep headphone volume at a comfortable level to avoid distortion and hearing damage.

**Monitor Mix:** If recording with multiple hosts or guests remotely, ensure everyone can hear each other clearly through headphones.

## 4.3.5 Recording Levels and Gain

PROPERLY SETTING RECORDING levels and gain ensures your audio isn't too quiet or distorted:

**Optimal Levels**

Aim for peak audio levels between -6dB and -3dB to leave headroom for unexpected loud sounds.

**Gain Control**

Adjust the microphone's gain or input level to achieve the desired recording levels. Be cautious not to set it too high, as it may lead to distortion.

**Test Recordings**

Conduct test recordings and monitor the audio levels to fine-tune gain settings.

## 4.3.6 Redundancy and Backups

MINIMIZE THE RISK OF losing your recordings due to technical issues:

**Backup Recordings**

Consider using dual recording systems or recording backups to ensure you have a copy of your audio in case of equipment failure.

**Regular Backups**

Immediately back up your recordings after each session to prevent data loss.

## 4.3.7 Pacing and Delivery

EFFECTIVE PACING AND delivery enhance listener engagement:

☑ **Speak Clearly:** Enunciate your words and speak at a moderate pace to ensure your audience can understand you.

☑ **Pauses:** Use strategic pauses to emphasize points, allow for breathing, and facilitate editing.

☑ **Energy and Enthusiasm:** Convey enthusiasm and energy in your delivery to keep your audience engaged.

## 4.3.8 Scripting and Notes

PLANNING YOUR CONTENT with scripts and notes can help you stay on track:

**Scripting:** Write a script for your podcast episodes to ensure a clear structure and message.

**Episode Outlines:** Use episode outlines or bullet points to guide the conversation and stay organized.

## 4.3.9 Editing Considerations

WHILE POST-PRODUCTION is essential, aim to capture clean audio during recording:

**Edit Lightly:** Minimize the need for extensive editing by capturing high-quality audio from the start.

**Backup Recordings:** Keep backup recordings in case of unexpected issues during editing.

## 4.3.10 Etiquette and Communication

MAINTAIN PROFESSIONALISM and clear communication with co-hosts or guests:

**Turn-Taking:** Establish clear turn-taking and speaking order to prevent overlapping conversations.

**Non-Verbal Cues:** Use non-verbal cues or signals (e.g., hand gestures or eye contact) to coordinate discussions.

Recording techniques and best practices play a pivotal role in achieving professional-quality podcast audio. By carefully selecting equipment, optimizing microphone placement, creating a suitable recording environment, and following essential guidelines, you'll be well on your way to capturing exceptional podcast recordings.

# 4.4: Editing and Post-Production

―――

O nce you've recorded your podcast, the next crucial step is editing and post-production. This chapter delves into the techniques, tools, and best practices to transform your raw audio recordings into polished, professional episodes.

## 4.4.1 Essential Editing Tools and Software

BEFORE DIVING INTO the editing process, familiarize yourself with the essential tools and software:

### Digital Audio Workstations (DAWs)

Choose a DAW that suits your needs, such as Adobe Audition, Audacity (free), Reaper, GarageBand (for Mac users), or Pro Tools.

### Audio Plugins

Explore audio plugins for enhancing audio quality, noise reduction, equalization, and special effects. Common plugins include iZotope RX, Waves plugins, and FabFilter.

### Editing Hardware

Consider using a high-quality set of headphones, a digital audio interface, and a reliable computer to handle your editing tasks efficiently.

## 4.4.2 Editing Workflow

DEVELOP A STRUCTURED editing workflow to streamline your post-production process:

### File Organization

Create a well-organized folder structure for your podcast episodes, including raw audio files, project files, and assets like music and sound effects.

### Importing and Syncing

Import your recorded audio tracks into the DAW, sync multiple tracks if needed, and label them clearly.

### Editing Timeline

Arrange your audio tracks on a timeline, starting with the intro, main content, and outro segments.

### Removing Mistakes

Carefully edit out any mistakes, long pauses, background noise, or irrelevant content. Use editing tools like cut, copy, paste, and silence to refine the audio.

### Smooth Transitions

Ensure smooth transitions between segments and topics by using crossfades or fade-in/fade-out effects.

### Adding Music and Sound Effects

Incorporate background music, intro/outro music, and relevant sound effects to enhance the listening experience.

### Balancing Levels

Adjust the volume levels to maintain consistency throughout the episode. Use compression and limiting to control dynamic range.

### Equalization (EQ)

Apply EQ to improve clarity and tone. Address issues like excessive bass or harsh treble frequencies.

### Noise Reduction

Employ noise reduction tools to minimize background noise and unwanted hums or hisses.

**Editing for Clarity**

Focus on clarity in speech by removing mouth noises (clicks, pops, and saliva sounds) and excessive breaths.

**Correction and Enhancement**

Correct minor recording issues, like off-mic moments or mic plosives, and enhance overall audio quality.

## 4.4.3 Special Effects and Enhancements

EXPLORE CREATIVE POSSIBILITIES through special effects and enhancements:

**Adding Reverb and Echo:** Use reverb and echo effects for a spacious or dramatic feel in storytelling or narration.

**Pitch and Time Manipulation:** Experiment with pitch shifting or time-stretching for creative effects or to adjust pacing.

**Sound Design:** Create custom soundscapes or atmospheric effects to enrich your storytelling.

**Binaural and Spatial Audio:** Explore spatial audio techniques to immerse listeners in a 3D auditory experience.

## 4.4.4 Review and Quality Assurance

THOROUGHLY REVIEW AND quality-check your edited episode:

☐ **Listening Session:** Listen to the entire episode with a critical ear to identify any remaining issues.

☐ **Proofreading:** Check for any script discrepancies, factual errors, or mispronunciations.

☐ **Audio Checks:** Ensure that all audio elements are correctly synchronized and free of glitches.

☐ **Consistency:** Verify that the episode maintains a consistent tone, volume level, and overall quality.

## 4.4.5 Exporting and File Formats

PREPARE YOUR EPISODE for distribution by exporting it in the appropriate file format:

**File Format:** Common formats for podcast episodes include MP3, WAV, and FLAC. Choose the one that best balances audio quality and file size.

**Bitrate:** Set an optimal bitrate for your chosen format to maintain audio quality while keeping file sizes manageable.

**ID3 Tags**: Embed ID3 tags, including episode title, artist, album, and cover art, into your MP3 files for proper podcast metadata.

## 4.4.6 Creating Show Notes and Metadata

GENERATE ENGAGING SHOW notes and metadata to accompany your podcast episode:

**Show Notes:** Craft comprehensive show notes that summarize the episode, provide timestamps, and include relevant links and resources.

**Metadata Optimization:** Optimize your episode's metadata, including title, description, keywords, and episode number, to improve discoverability on podcast platforms.

## 4.4.7 Final Quality Check

BEFORE PUBLISHING, perform a final quality check:

☑ **Listen Again:** Listen to the fully edited episode once more to ensure everything is in place and sounds impeccable.

☑ **Volume Levels:** Double-check volume levels to prevent any unexpected audio discrepancies.

☑ **Metadata Review:** Verify that all metadata is accurate and up to date.

## 4.4.8 Backup and Archiving

MAINTAIN BACKUPS OF your edited episodes and project files:

**Backup Storage:** Regularly back up your edited episodes and project files to external drives or cloud storage to prevent

# 4.5: Adding Music and Sound Effects

———

Music and sound effects are powerful tools in podcast production, enhancing the overall listening experience, setting the mood, and adding depth to your content. This chapter explores how to effectively incorporate music and sound effects into your podcast.

## 4.5.1 Choosing the Right Music and Sound Effects

SELECTING THE APPROPRIATE music and sound effects is crucial to complement your podcast's theme and narrative:

**Genre and Style**

Consider the genre and style of music that aligns with your podcast's tone. Whether it's classical, jazz, rock, electronic, or royalty-free music, ensure it fits the content.

**Copyright and Licensing**

Pay attention to copyright and licensing regulations. Use royalty-free or licensed music to avoid legal issues. Platforms like Epidemic Sound, PremiumBeat, or Audiojungle offer vast libraries of music.

**Original Compositions**

If possible, collaborate with composers or musicians to create original music that is tailored to your podcast's unique identity.

**Sound Effects Libraries**

Utilize sound effects libraries like Freesound.org, Sound Bible, or the BBC Sound Effects Library for a wide range of sound effects.

## 4.5.2 Introducing Music and Sound Effects

INCORPORATE MUSIC AND sound effects effectively into your podcast:

### Intro and Outro Music

Create a memorable introduction and outro for your podcast with music that reflects its personality. Consistency in these elements helps establish your podcast's brand.

### Transitions

Use transitional music or sound effects to smoothly move between segments, creating a cohesive listening experience.

### Emotional Impact

Enhance emotional moments or storytelling elements with music that resonates with your audience.

### Soundscapes

Create immersive soundscapes by layering background music or ambient sounds to transport your listeners to different settings.

## 4.5.3 Audio Mixing and Balancing

MAINTAIN A BALANCED audio mix when incorporating music and sound effects:

### Volume Levels

Ensure that music and sound effects don't overpower the primary audio, such as speech. Adjust volume levels to maintain clarity.

### Equalization (EQ)

Apply EQ to music and sound effects to avoid frequency clashes with voice recordings. This prevents muddiness in the audio.

### Panning

Experiment with panning to position music and sound effects spatially in the stereo field for a more dynamic listening experience.

## 4.5.4 Timing and Synchronization

TIMING IS CRITICAL when introducing music and sound effects:

### Sync with Content

Align music and sound effects with the content they enhance. For example, add suspenseful music during suspenseful moments or punctuate jokes with well-timed sound effects.

### Transitions

Smoothly transition in and out of music or sound effects to avoid abrupt disruptions.

### Rhythmic Elements

Leverage the rhythm and tempo of music to match the pacing of your podcast.

## 4.5.5 Licensing and Attribution

RESPECT LICENSING AND attribution requirements when using music and sound effects:

### Royalty-Free Licensing

If you use royalty-free music, understand the terms of use and any attribution requirements specified by the provider.

### Attribution

When necessary, provide proper attribution for the music or sound effects you use. Include this information in your episode's credits or show notes.

## 4.5.6 Creating Original Music and Sound Effects

FOR A UNIQUE PODCAST identity, consider creating your own music and sound effects:

**DIY Music**

Compose original music or collaborate with musicians to craft bespoke pieces that align perfectly with your podcast's theme.

**Custom Sound Effects**

Record and edit your own sound effects to ensure they match your content's needs precisely.

## 4.5.7 Testing and Feedback

BEFORE FINALIZING MUSIC and sound effects in your episodes, gather feedback:

**Listening Panel:** Assemble a listening panel to review episodes with music and sound effects. Collect constructive feedback to refine your audio choices.

**Audience Input:** Encourage your audience to provide feedback on the use of music and sound effects through surveys or social media engagement.

## 4.5.8 Post-Production Quality Control

DURING THE EDITING phase, conduct a quality check focused on music and sound effects:

> **Audio Levels:** Double-check that music and sound effects are appropriately leveled to prevent audio imbalances.

> **Consistency:** Ensure that the style, tone, and volume of music and sound effects remain consistent throughout the episode.

> **Eliminate Clutter:** Remove any unnecessary or distracting music or sound effects that do not contribute to the listening experience.

## 4.5.9 Copyright Compliance and Documentation

MAINTAIN DOCUMENTATION and proof of licensing for all music and sound effects used:

**File Organization:** Organize your music and sound effects library with clear filenames and folder structures, including licensing details.

**Licensing Records:** Keep records of licenses, attributions, and permissions for each.

# Chapter 5: Editing and Polishing

# Chapter 5.1: Audio Editing Software and Tools

―――

A udio editing is a fundamental aspect of podcast production, shaping the final sound and quality of your episodes. This chapter explores the essential software and tools needed for audio editing and provides insights into their effective usage.

## 5.1.1 Digital Audio Workstations (DAWs)

DIGITAL AUDIO WORKSTATIONS (DAWs) are the core software tools for editing, processing, and mixing your podcast audio. Choosing the right DAW is crucial for a seamless editing experience:

### Adobe Audition

Known for its powerful audio editing capabilities, Adobe Audition offers a user-friendly interface and a wide range of features, making it suitable for both beginners and professionals.

### Audacity

As a free, open-source DAW, Audacity is accessible to all podcasters. It offers essential editing tools, making it a great starting point for those on a budget.

### Reaper

Reaper is a highly customizable and affordable DAW favored by many podcasters. Its extensive features and plugin compatibility make it a versatile choice.

### GarageBand

Exclusively for Mac users, GarageBand provides a straightforward, beginner-friendly platform for audio editing and podcast production.

## Pro Tools

Often used in professional studios, Pro Tools offers advanced capabilities for podcasters seeking the highest quality and precision.

## 5.1.2 Audio Plugins and Effects

ENHANCE YOUR PODCAST audio quality and creativity by incorporating audio plugins and effects into your editing workflow:

### EQ Plugins

Equalization (EQ) plugins allow you to adjust the frequency balance of your audio, improving clarity and removing unwanted noise.

### Compression Plugins

Compression plugins help control the dynamic range of your podcast audio, ensuring that loud and soft parts are balanced.

### Noise Reduction

Noise reduction plugins are essential for eliminating background noise, hums, or hisses, resulting in cleaner audio.

### Reverb and Delay

These effects can add depth and atmosphere to your podcast, simulating various acoustic environments or creating unique sonic textures.

### Special Effects

Explore creative plugins for sound design, such as distortion, chorus, and pitch-shifting, to experiment with your podcast's audio.

### Vocal Processing

Plugins designed for vocal processing can enhance voice recordings, providing a polished and professional sound.

## 5.1.3 Essential Editing Techniques

MASTERING THE FUNDAMENTAL editing techniques is key to producing high-quality podcast episodes:

☑ **Cut and Trim:** Remove unwanted sections, pauses, mistakes, or background noise by cutting and trimming audio clips.

☑ **Crossfades and Transitions:** Smoothly blend segments or clips using crossfades, ensuring seamless transitions.

☑ **Volume Adjustments:** Maintain consistent audio levels by adjusting the volume throughout the episode.

☑ **Panning:** Position audio elements in the stereo field to create a sense of space and direction.

☑ **Timing and Synchronization:** Ensure that audio elements, such as music, sound effects, and dialogue, are synchronized correctly.

☑ **Fade-ins and Fade-outs:** Use fade-ins and fade-outs to gently introduce or conclude audio clips.

☑ **Time Stretching:** Adjust the timing of audio clips to match the desired pacing of your podcast.

## 5.1.4 Noise Reduction and Restoration

TO ACHIEVE PRISTINE audio quality, employ noise reduction and restoration techniques:

**Noise Reduction Tools**

DAWs often include built-in noise reduction tools that can intelligently remove background noise without affecting the main audio.

**Spectral Editing**

Advanced spectral editing allows you to target and remove specific frequencies associated with noise, clicks, or hums.

**De-essing**

Address sibilance issues by using de-essing plugins to reduce harsh "s" and "sh" sounds.

**Restoration**

Repair damaged or distorted audio using restoration plugins and techniques to salvage valuable recordings.

## 5.1.5 Multitrack Editing

MULTITRACK EDITING is essential for managing multiple audio sources, such as interviews, music, and sound effects:

- **Track Organization:** Keep your project organized by assigning each audio source to a separate track for easy manipulation.

- **Track Effects:** Apply specific effects and adjustments to individual tracks, tailoring the processing to each source's requirements.

- **Mixing:** Achieve the perfect balance between different audio sources through mixing, ensuring that all elements are clearly audible.

## 5.1.6 Recording Corrections

CORRECTING ISSUES DURING the editing process is a standard practice:

★ **Removing Mouth Noises:** Edit out distracting mouth noises, like clicks, pops, or excessive lip smacks, to improve clarity.

★ **Plosive Removal:** Address plosives (explosive sounds like "p" and "b") using editing techniques or dedicated plugins.

★ **Breath Control:** Reduce heavy or distracting breathing sounds while maintaining natural breaths for a polished result.

## 5.1.7 Exporting and File Formats

PREPARE YOUR EDITED podcast audio for distribution with proper export settings:

❖ **File Formats:** Common formats for podcast audio include MP3, WAV, and FLAC. Select the format that balances audio quality and file size.

❖ **Bitrate:** Set an optimal bitrate for your chosen format to maintain audio quality while keeping file sizes manageable.

❖ **Metadata:** Embed metadata, including episode title, artist, album, and cover art, into your audio files to provide essential information to listeners and podcast platforms.

## 5.1.8 Backups and Version Control

MAINTAIN BACKUPS AND version control to safeguard your edited audio and project files:

### Backup Storage

Regularly back up your edited episodes and project files to external drives or cloud storage to prevent data loss.

### Version Control

Implement version control practices to track changes and revisions in your editing process, ensuring you can revert to previous states if needed.

## 5.1.9 Collaboration and Review

COLLABORATING WITH a team or seeking feedback can help improve your podcast's audio quality:

**Team Collaboration**

If you work with a team, establish clear communication and collaboration workflows to streamline the editing process.

**Peer Review**

Have colleagues or peers review your edited episodes for constructive feedback and quality assurance.

**Listener Feedback**

Encourage your audience to provide feedback on audio quality and content delivery, addressing any issues or concerns raised.

## 5.1.10 Accessibility Considerations

ENSURE THAT YOUR EDITED audio content is accessible to all listeners:

**Transcripts**

Provide transcripts or captions for your episodes to make them accessible to individuals with hearing impairments or those who prefer reading.

**Audio Description**

Consider adding audio descriptions for visual content within your podcast to enhance accessibility for visually impaired listeners.

## 5.1.11 Copyright and Licensing Compliance

RESPECT COPYRIGHT AND licensing regulations when using third-party audio elements:

**Licensed Music**

If you use copyrighted music, obtain the necessary licenses and permissions to avoid legal issues.

**Attribution**

Provide proper attribution for any licensed or royalty-free audio elements, following the requirements specified by the creator or provider.

## 5.1.12 Final Quality Assurance

BEFORE PUBLISHING, conduct a final quality assurance check:

**Listening Session**

Listen to the fully edited episode from start to finish, noting any remaining audio issues or discrepancies.

**Volume Levels**

Ensure that all audio elements, including dialogue, music, and sound effects, are appropriately balanced for consistent listening.

**Metadata Review**

Verify that metadata, such as episode titles, descriptions, and episode numbers

# 5.2: Cleaning Up Audio Quality

———

A udio quality is paramount in podcasting. This chapter delves into essential techniques and tools for cleaning up your podcast audio to achieve professional and pristine sound.

## 5.2.1 Identifying Common Audio Issues

BEFORE DIVING INTO the cleaning process, it's essential to recognize common audio issues that may arise during podcast recording:

☐ **Background Noise:** Unwanted ambient sounds like air conditioning, traffic, or computer fans can detract from audio quality.

☐ **Mouth Noises:** Clicks, pops, and lip-smacking sounds can be distracting to listeners.

☐ **Plosives:** Explosive sounds produced by words like "p" and "b" can create unpleasant audio spikes.

☐ **Sibilance:** Harsh "s" and "sh" sounds can be abrasive to the ears.

☐ **Uneven Volume Levels:** Inconsistent speaking volumes or variations in microphone technique can result in uneven audio.

## 5.2.2 Noise Reduction and Removal

NOISE REDUCTION IS a crucial step in improving audio quality:

**Noise Reduction Plugins**

Digital Audio Workstations (DAWs) often provide noise reduction plugins that can intelligently identify and reduce background noise.

**Manual Noise Removal**

In cases where noise reduction plugins may not suffice, manual noise removal techniques involve selecting portions of audio containing noise and reducing their volume or applying spectral editing to remove specific frequencies.

**Recording Techniques**

Preventing noise at the source through proper microphone placement, acoustic treatment, and sound isolation can reduce the need for extensive noise reduction.

## 5.2.3 Mouth Noise and Plosive Removal

ELIMINATING DISTRACTING mouth noises and plosives enhances clarity:

**Editing Tools**

Use editing tools in your DAW to carefully remove or reduce mouth noises and plosives. These tools allow you to select and adjust specific audio segments.

**De-essing**

De-essing plugins are effective for addressing sibilance, reducing harsh "s" and "sh" sounds without affecting the overall audio.

**Pop Filters and Windscreens**

Employ pop filters and windscreens during recording to minimize plosives at the source.

## 5.2.4 Volume Leveling and Compression

ACHIEVING CONSISTENT volume levels throughout your podcast is crucial:

**Volume Automation**

Use volume automation to manually adjust audio levels, ensuring a consistent listening experience.

**Compression**

Apply compression to control dynamic range and prevent sudden volume spikes or drops. Compressors are essential tools for leveling audio.

**Multiband Compression**

For more precise control, consider multiband compression to target specific frequency ranges.

## 5.2.5 Equalization (EQ) and Frequency Balancing

EQ HELPS IN SHAPING your audio and addressing tonal issues:

**Voice Enhancement**

Apply EQ to enhance vocal clarity and remove frequency imbalances. Boosting or cutting specific frequencies can improve overall sound quality.

**High-Pass and Low-Pass Filters**

Use high-pass filters to remove low-frequency rumble and low-pass filters to attenuate excessive high-frequency noise.

**Spectral Editing**

In cases where standard EQ may not suffice, spectral editing tools allow for precise adjustments by visualizing audio frequencies.

## 5.2.6 De-Clipping and Restoration

AUDIO CLIPPING, WHICH occurs when the recording level exceeds the maximum capacity of the microphone or recording device, can result in distorted audio. De-clipping tools can help restore clipped audio segments.

## 5.2.7 Handling Reverb and Echo

REVERB AND ECHO CAN negatively impact audio quality. Addressing these issues may require specialized tools or acoustic treatment:

**De-Reverberation**

Some DAWs offer de-reverberation plugins to reduce excessive reverb in audio recordings.

**Acoustic Treatment**

Improve recording environments by incorporating acoustic treatment materials like bass traps and diffusers to minimize reverb and echo.

## 5.2.8 Rescuing Overly Compressed Audio

IN SOME CASES, AUDIO may arrive already compressed or overly processed. Techniques like "parallel compression" or "upward expansion" can help salvage such audio.

## 5.2.9 Manual Editing and Restoration

EXTENSIVE MANUAL EDITING may be necessary for specific issues:

**Clicks and Pops**

Manually remove clicks and pops using editing tools or spectral editing techniques.

**Crossfades**

Apply crossfades to create smooth transitions between edited segments, avoiding abrupt changes in audio.

## 5.2.10 Listener Feedback and Iteration

GATHER FEEDBACK FROM listeners to identify recurring audio quality concerns. Use this feedback to iteratively improve your recording and editing techniques.

## 5.2.11 Quality Assurance and Testing

BEFORE FINALIZING AN episode, conduct quality assurance checks:

**Listening Sessions**

Listen to the entire episode with headphones, paying attention to audio quality and potential issues.

**Peer Review**

Have colleagues or peers review the audio for additional insights and feedback.

## 5.2.12 Backup and Version Control

ALWAYS MAINTAIN BACKUPS of your raw audio recordings and edited files to prevent data loss during the editing and cleaning process.

## 5.2.13 Accessibility Considerations

CONSIDER THE ACCESSIBILITY of your podcast by providing transcripts or captions for listeners with hearing impairments or those who prefer reading.

## 5.2.14 Copyright and Licensing Compliance

ENSURE THAT ANY AUDIO elements used in your podcast, such as music or sound effects, comply with copyright and licensing regulations.

## 5.2.15 Final Quality Assurance Check

BEFORE PUBLISHING YOUR episode, perform a final quality assurance check:

☑ **Listen Again:** Carefully listen to the fully edited episode from start to finish, noting any remaining audio issues or discrepancies.

☑ **Volume Levels:** Confirm that all audio elements, including dialogue, music, and sound effects, are appropriately balanced for a consistent listening experience.

☑ **Metadata Review:** Verify that metadata, such as episode titles, descriptions, and episode numbers, accurately reflects the content of the episode.

By following these guidelines and techniques, you can elevate the audio quality of your podcast, delivering a professional and enjoyable listening experience to your audience.

# 5.3: Enhancing Sound with Effects

—

S ound effects are a powerful tool in podcasting. They can elevate your content, immerse your listeners, and add depth to your storytelling. This chapter explores various sound effects and how to use them effectively.

## 5.3.1 Understanding Sound Effects

SOUND EFFECTS, OFTEN abbreviated as SFX, are sounds that are artificially created or recorded to enhance audio content. They can range from subtle background ambiance to dramatic, attention-grabbing effects. Understanding the types of sound effects and their roles is essential:

**Ambient Effects**

These create a sense of place or atmosphere, such as the sounds of a bustling café, a forest at night, or a busy city street.

**Foley Effects**

Foley artists recreate real-world sounds, like footsteps on different surfaces, doors creaking, or objects being handled.

**Impact Effects**

These are used to emphasize actions or events, like punches, crashes, or explosions.

**Transition Effects**

Transition sound effects smooth out audio transitions, such as scene changes or time shifts.

**Emotional Effects**

These effects evoke emotions or moods, like laughter, suspenseful music, or applause.

## 5.3.2 Selecting Appropriate Sound Effects

CHOOSING THE RIGHT sound effects is crucial for enhancing your podcast:

### Relevance

Ensure that the selected sound effects are relevant to the content and context of your podcast. Irrelevant or excessive effects can distract and annoy listeners.

### Tone and Mood

Consider the emotional tone and mood you want to convey. Sound effects should align with the intended atmosphere of your podcast.

### Balance

Strike a balance between the narrative and the sound effects. They should complement each other, not compete for attention.

## 5.3.3 Sourcing Sound Effects

YOU CAN ACQUIRE SOUND effects from various sources:

### Online Libraries

Numerous online platforms offer sound effect libraries with a wide range of options. Some are free, while others require a subscription or one-time purchase.

### DIY Recording

Create your sound effects by recording sounds using a microphone. This approach allows for custom effects tailored to your podcast's unique needs.

### Public Domain

Some sound effects are in the public domain and can be used freely. Ensure you verify the licensing and attribution requirements.

### Licensed Effects

Purchase licenses for specific sound effects when necessary, especially for commercial or proprietary use.

## 5.3.4 Integrating Sound Effects

EFFECTIVELY INTEGRATING sound effects into your podcast is an art:

### Timing

The timing of sound effects is crucial. They should enhance the listener's experience and synchronize with the narrative.

### Volume Control

Adjust the volume of sound effects to ensure they are audible but not overpowering. Use automation tools in your Digital Audio Workstation (DAW) for precise control.

### Layering

Combine multiple sound effects to create depth and richness in your audio. Layering can add realism and dimension to your podcast.

## 5.3.5 Music and Soundtrack

INCORPORATING MUSIC and soundtracks is another way to enhance your podcast:

### Background Music

Choose background music that complements your podcast's theme and mood. Ensure it doesn't interfere with dialogue or narration.

### Transitions

Use musical cues to signal transitions between segments or scenes, creating a cohesive listening experience.

### Custom Composition

Consider commissioning custom music or soundtracks tailored to your podcast for a unique and memorable sound.

## 5.3.6 Creating Consistency

MAINTAINING CONSISTENCY in your use of sound effects is essential:

### Establish Patterns

Create patterns for recurring elements or segments, such as intro/outro music, transitions, or recurring themes.

### Style Guide

Develop a style guide for your podcast's audio, including guidelines for the use of sound effects, music, and volume levels.

## 5.3.7 Listener Experience

PRIORITIZE THE LISTENER'S experience when using sound effects:

### Testing

Always test your podcast with sound effects on different listening devices to ensure they sound as intended.

### Listener Feedback

Encourage listener feedback and pay attention to their opinions on sound effects. Adjust your approach based on their input.

## 5.3.8 Copyright and Licensing

BE AWARE OF COPYRIGHT and licensing issues related to sound effects:

### Royalty-Free

Opt for royalty-free or licensed sound effects to avoid legal complications. Understand the terms of use and attribution requirements.

**Creative Commons**

Some sound effects are available under Creative Commons licenses, each with its own usage conditions.

## 5.3.9 Accessibility Considerations

REMEMBER TO MAKE YOUR podcast accessible to all listeners, including those with hearing impairments. Provide transcripts or descriptions of sound effects when necessary.

## 5.3.10 Final Review and Quality Assurance

BEFORE PUBLISHING YOUR podcast episode, conduct a final review to ensure that sound effects enhance the overall quality and storytelling without overwhelming or distracting your audience

# 5.4: Balancing and Equalizing Audio

Balancing and equalizing audio is a critical step in the podcast production process. These techniques ensure that your podcast sounds clear, professional, and well-suited for your audience. In this chapter, we'll explore the intricacies of audio balancing and equalization.

## 5.4.1 Balancing Audio Levels

BALANCING AUDIO LEVELS involves adjusting the volume of different audio elements within your podcast to achieve a harmonious mix. Properly balanced audio ensures that no element, such as voices, music, or sound effects, overpowers the others. Here's how to master audio balancing:

☑ **Voice Clarity:** Your podcast's primary focus should be the spoken content. Ensure that the voices of your hosts or guests are clear and easily understood.

☑ **Music Integration:** If your podcast includes music, balance it carefully with the voices. The music should enhance the content without drowning out the dialogue.

☑ **Sound Effects:** Ensure that sound effects are at an appropriate volume. They should enhance the listening experience without becoming distracting.

☑ **Volume Consistency:** Maintain consistent volume levels throughout your podcast. Sudden volume spikes or drops can frustrate listeners.

☑ **Automation Tools:** Use automation features in your Digital Audio Workstation (DAW) to adjust volume levels smoothly, particularly during transitions.

## 5.4.2 Equalizing Audio

EQUALIZATION, OFTEN referred to as EQ, involves adjusting the frequency balance of your podcast's audio. It allows you to enhance clarity, correct imperfections, and create a pleasing auditory experience. Consider the following aspects of audio equalization:

**Frequency Bands**

Understand the different frequency bands, including bass (low frequencies), midrange (mid frequencies), and treble (high frequencies). Each band contributes to the overall sound.

**Voice Enhancement**

Use EQ to accentuate the clarity of voices. This might involve boosting midrange frequencies where speech is most prominent.

**Removing Noise**

EQ can help reduce unwanted background noise or hum by cutting or attenuating specific frequencies.

**Balancing Instruments**

If your podcast features musical instruments, EQ can help balance their tones within the mix.

**Voice Consistency**

Ensure that the voices of different hosts or guests sound consistent in terms of tonal quality.

**Audio Correction**

Correct any anomalies or imperfections in the audio, such as excessive sibilance (harsh "s" sounds) or plosives (popped "p" sounds).

**Applying Presets**

Many DAWs offer EQ presets for various scenarios. Experiment with these presets to find the one that best suits your podcast's needs.

### 5.4.3 Graphic vs. Parametric EQ

THERE ARE TWO PRIMARY types of EQ used in podcasting:

❖ **Graphic EQ:** Graphic equalizers allow you to adjust predefined frequency bands using sliders or knobs. They are user-friendly and provide a visual representation of adjustments.

❖ **Parametric EQ:** Parametric equalizers offer more precise control, allowing you to adjust specific frequencies, bandwidth, and gain. They are ideal for fine-tuning audio.

### 5.4.4 EQ Tips and Techniques

MASTERING EQUALIZATION requires skill and practice. Here are some essential tips and techniques:

☐ **Frequency Analysis:** Use a frequency analyzer to identify frequency spikes or imbalances in your audio.

☐ **Subtractive EQ:** Begin with subtractive EQ by reducing problematic frequencies before boosting others.

☐ **Surgical EQ:** For problematic sounds or voices, consider surgical EQ to target and remove specific unwanted frequencies.

☐ **High-Pass and Low-Pass Filters:** Employ high-pass filters to remove low-frequency rumble and low-pass filters to reduce high-frequency noise.

☐ **Avoid Overdoing It:** Be cautious about excessive equalization. Small adjustments can yield significant improvements.

☐ **Test and Listen:** Continuously test your podcast's audio on various playback devices to ensure it sounds great everywhere.

## 5.4.5 Presets and Plugins

EXPLORE EQ PRESETS and plugins to simplify the equalization process:

**Presets**

Many DAWs offer EQ presets tailored for different audio scenarios, such as podcasts or voiceovers.

**Third-Party Plugins**

Consider using third-party EQ plugins that offer advanced features and customization options.

## 5.4.6 Monitoring and Feedback

REGULARLY MONITOR YOUR audio during recording, editing, and mixing. Seek feedback from trusted listeners or colleagues to fine-tune your audio balancing and equalization techniques.

## 5.4.7 Final Quality Check

BEFORE PUBLISHING YOUR podcast episode, conduct a final quality check to ensure that audio balancing and equalization have been applied effectively. Listen critically to the entire episode to catch any inconsistencies or issues.

# 5.5: Adding Intro and Outro

The introduction (intro) and conclusion (outro) segments of your podcast are like bookends that frame your content. They serve essential purposes, such as engaging listeners from the start and providing a memorable closing. In this chapter, we'll delve into the art of creating compelling intros and outros for your podcast.

## 5.5.1 Crafting an Engaging Podcast Introduction (Intro)

YOUR PODCAST'S INTRODUCTION is your first opportunity to captivate your audience. A well-crafted intro can set the tone, pique curiosity, and establish a connection with listeners. Consider the following elements for creating an engaging intro:

❖ **Hooking the Audience:** Begin with a hook that grabs the listener's attention. This can be a thought-provoking question, an intriguing fact, or a compelling statement related to your podcast's topic.

❖ **Identifying the Show:** Clearly state the name of your podcast. This helps listeners recognize and remember your brand.

❖ **Introducing the Host:** If you have a host or hosts, introduce them briefly. Provide a concise bio or highlight their credentials to build credibility.

❖ **Teasing the Content:** Give listeners a glimpse of what to expect in the episode. Offer a brief overview of the topics, guests, or key points you'll cover.

❖ **Setting the Vibe:** Match the tone and style of your intro to the overall mood of your podcast. Whether it's lighthearted, informative, or dramatic, ensure consistency.

❖ **Including Music or Sound Effects:** Consider incorporating music or sound effects that complement your podcast's theme. These elements can enhance the emotional impact of your intro.

## 5.5.2 Structuring an Effective Podcast Outro

THE OUTRO OF YOUR PODCAST provides closure and leaves a lasting impression on your audience. It's an opportunity to reinforce your podcast's identity, encourage engagement, and prepare listeners for what comes next. Here's how to structure an effective outro:

☑ **Expressing Gratitude:** Start by expressing gratitude to your listeners for tuning in. Show appreciation for their time and support.

☑ **Recap and Highlights:** Summarize the key points or highlights of the episode. This reinforces the value of your content.

☑ **Promoting Engagement:** Encourage listeners to take action, such as subscribing, leaving reviews, or sharing the podcast with friends. Provide clear calls to action (CTAs).

☑ **Teasing Future Content:** Offer a teaser or hint about what's coming up in future episodes. This can build anticipation and keep listeners engaged.

☑ **Including Contact Information:** Share how listeners can connect with you, whether through social media, email, or your website. Make it easy for them to reach out.

☑ **Using Music or Sound Effects:** Similar to the intro, consider adding music or sound effects to enhance the outro and create a memorable closing.

### 5.5.3 Finding the Right Balance

STRIKE A BALANCE BETWEEN brevity and informativeness in your intros and outros. While they should be concise, they should also provide enough context and value to engage your audience.

### 5.5.4 Scripting vs. Ad-Libbing

DECIDE WHETHER YOU'LL script your intros and outros or ad-lib them. Some podcasters prefer the spontaneity of ad-libbing, while others opt for scripted segments for precision.

### 5.5.5 Consistency and Branding

MAINTAIN CONSISTENCY in your intros and outros across episodes. Consistency helps in branding and makes your podcast recognizable. Consider using similar music, tone, and style.

### 5.5.6 Editing and Post-Production

PAY ATTENTION TO EDITING and post-production to ensure that your intros and outros are seamless and free of technical glitches or interruptions.

### 5.5.7 Listener Feedback

GATHER FEEDBACK FROM your listeners about your intros and outros. Their insights can help you refine and improve these segments over time.

### 5.5.8 Examples and Inspiration

LISTEN TO SUCCESSFUL podcasts in your niche or genre to get inspiration for effective intros and outros. Analyze what works well and adapt those elements to your podcast.

### 5.5.9 Final Review and Testing

BEFORE FINALIZING YOUR intros and outros, conduct a review and testing phase. Listen to them multiple times to ensure they align with your podcast's goals and effectively engage your audience.

### 5.5.10 Evolution and Adaptation

BE OPEN TO EVOLVING your intros and outros as your podcast grows and changes. Adapt them to match shifting content, audience preferences, and your evolving podcasting journey.

Crafting engaging intros and outros is an art that can significantly enhance the overall quality of your podcast. These segments serve as the welcoming and closing gestures of your podcasting journey, leaving a lasting impression on your listeners.

# Chapter 6: Publishing and Distribution

In the dynamic world of podcasting, publishing and distribution are crucial steps in getting your content into the ears of your audience. This chapter explores the essential aspects of choosing the right podcast hosting platform, distributing your episodes effectively, and maximizing your podcast's reach.

# 6.1 Choosing a Podcast Hosting Platform

---

S electing the appropriate podcast hosting platform is fundamental to the success of your podcast. It's the platform where your episodes will be stored, managed, and distributed to various podcast directories and platforms. Consider the following factors when choosing a podcast hosting platform:

## 6.1.1 Features and Capabilities

EVALUATE THE FEATURES and capabilities offered by different hosting platforms. Look for essential features such as unlimited storage, bandwidth, analytics, customization options, scheduling tools, and monetization opportunities. Consider whether the platform supports video podcasting, live streaming, or other advanced features that align with your podcasting goals.

## 6.1.2 Pricing and Plans

COMPARE THE PRICING plans of different hosting platforms to find one that fits your budget and requirements. Look for transparent pricing with no hidden fees and consider whether the platform offers a free trial or a tiered pricing structure that scales with your podcast's growth. Take into account any additional costs for premium features or upgrades.

## 6.1.3 User Interface and Ease of Use

CHOOSE A HOSTING PLATFORM with an intuitive user interface and easy-to-use tools. The platform should streamline the process of uploading, managing, and publishing your episodes, allowing you to focus on creating content rather than grappling with technical complexities. Look for platforms with responsive customer support and robust documentation to assist you when needed.

### 6.1.4 Distribution and Syndication

ENSURE THAT THE HOSTING platform provides seamless distribution and syndication of your episodes to popular podcast directories and platforms such as Apple Podcasts, Spotify, Google Podcasts, Stitcher, and others. Verify whether the platform offers automatic distribution, RSS feed generation, and integration with podcast directories to maximize your podcast's visibility and accessibility.

### 6.1.5 Monetization Options

CONSIDER THE MONETIZATION options available on the hosting platform, such as advertising, sponsorships, listener donations, premium content, or subscription models. Evaluate the platform's revenue-sharing policies, payment processing fees, and support for monetization strategies that align with your podcasting goals. Choose a platform that provides flexible monetization options to monetize your podcast effectively.

### 6.1.6 Analytics and Insights

LOOK FOR HOSTING PLATFORMS that offer robust analytics and insights to track your podcast's performance and audience engagement. Key metrics to consider include downloads, listens, audience demographics, listener retention, geographic distribution, and user engagement. Analyze these metrics to gain valuable insights into your audience's behavior and preferences, allowing you to refine your content and marketing strategies.

### 6.1.7 Scalability and Growth Potential

ANTICIPATE THE FUTURE growth of your podcast and choose a hosting platform that can scale with your needs. Consider whether the platform offers scalability features such as flexible storage and bandwidth options, advanced analytics, audience growth tools, and support for expanding your podcasting endeavors. Ensure that the platform can accommodate your podcast's growth without compromising performance or quality.

## 6.1.8 Reputation and Reliability

RESEARCH THE REPUTATION and reliability of hosting platforms by reading reviews, testimonials, and user feedback. Look for platforms with a track record of reliability, uptime, security, and customer satisfaction. Consider whether the platform has been endorsed or recommended by reputable podcasters or industry experts, indicating its credibility and trustworthiness.

## 6.1.9 Support and Community

EVALUATE THE LEVEL of support and community engagement offered by the hosting platform. Look for platforms that provide responsive customer support through various channels such as email, live chat, phone support, or community forums. Consider whether the platform offers resources, tutorials, webinars, or networking opportunities to help you succeed in your podcasting journey. Joining a supportive community of podcasters can provide valuable insights, advice, and collaboration opportunities.

## 6.1.10 Integration and Compatibility

ENSURE THAT THE HOSTING platform integrates seamlessly with other tools and services you use in your podcasting workflow, such as recording software, editing tools, social media platforms, email marketing software, and website builders. Verify whether the platform offers APIs, plugins, or integrations with third-party services to streamline your workflow and enhance productivity.

Choosing the right podcast hosting platform is a critical decision that impacts the success and growth of your podcast. By considering factors such as features, pricing, user interface, distribution, monetization options, analytics, scalability, reputation, support, and integration, you can find a hosting platform that meets your needs and empowers you to share your message with the world.

# 6.2 Creating Eye-Catching Cover Art

———

E ye-catching cover art is essential for attracting potential listeners and making a strong first impression in the crowded podcasting landscape. This section delves into the importance of cover art, key elements to consider when designing it, and best practices for creating compelling visuals that reflect your podcast's brand and content.

## 6.2.1 Importance of Cover Art

COVER ART SERVES AS the visual representation of your podcast and plays a crucial role in grabbing the attention of potential listeners browsing podcast directories. It serves as a visual cue that communicates the essence of your podcast's content, tone, and style at a glance. Eye-catching cover art can entice listeners to click on your podcast, while uninspiring or low-quality visuals may cause them to overlook it altogether.

## 6.2.2 Key Elements of Effective Cover Art

WHEN DESIGNING COVER art for your podcast, consider the following key elements to ensure it stands out and accurately represents your brand:

### Clear Branding

Ensure that your cover art reflects your podcast's brand identity, including its name, logo, colors, and typography. Consistent branding across all visual elements reinforces brand recognition and helps listeners identify your podcast amidst the sea of options available.

### Compelling Imagery

Choose imagery that aligns with your podcast's content, genre, and audience preferences. Use visually appealing graphics, illustrations, or photographs that capture the essence of your podcast's theme, whether it's educational, entertaining, informative, or thought-provoking.

## Legibility

Prioritize legibility by using clear and readable fonts for your podcast's title, subtitle, and any other text included in the cover art. Avoid overly intricate or decorative fonts that may be difficult to decipher, especially when displayed in smaller sizes on mobile devices.

## High-Quality Resolution

Ensure that your cover art is created and exported in high-resolution formats to maintain visual clarity and crispness across different devices and screen sizes. Low-resolution images can appear pixelated or blurry, detracting from the overall professionalism and appeal of your podcast.

## Visual Hierarchy

Establish a clear visual hierarchy within your cover art to guide viewers' attention and convey important information effectively. Use size, color, contrast, and positioning to emphasize key elements such as the podcast title, imagery, and branding elements.

## Consistency with Podcast Branding

Maintain consistency with your podcast's overall branding, including its visual style, tone, and messaging. Ensure that your cover art aligns with other branding assets such as your website, social media profiles, and promotional materials to create a cohesive and recognizable brand identity.

# 6.2.3 Best Practices for Designing Cover Art

FOLLOW THESE BEST PRACTICES when designing cover art for your podcast to maximize its visual impact and appeal:

## Research and Inspiration

Begin by researching existing podcast cover art within your niche or genre to identify trends, styles, and design elements that resonate with your target audience. Draw inspiration from successful podcasts while ensuring that your cover art remains unique and distinctive.

## Simplify and Focus

Keep your cover art simple and focused to avoid clutter and visual overload. Choose a central theme or focal point that encapsulates the essence of your podcast's content and eliminates unnecessary elements that may distract or confuse viewers.

## Test and Iterate

Test different iterations of your cover art by gathering feedback from peers, listeners, or focus groups. Pay attention to their reactions and suggestions for improvement and iterate on your designs accordingly to refine and optimize your cover art for maximum impact.

## Optimize for Different Platforms

Consider how your cover art will appear across various podcast directories, platforms, and devices, including desktops, smartphones, and tablets. Ensure that it remains visually compelling and legible at different sizes and resolutions to maintain consistency and accessibility.

## Stay on Brand

Stay true to your podcast's brand identity and messaging when designing cover art. Reflect your podcast's unique personality, tone, and values through your choice of imagery, colors, fonts, and visual style to create a cohesive and memorable brand experience for listeners.

## Seek Professional Assistance

Consider hiring a professional graphic designer or artist to create custom cover art for your podcast if you lack design skills or prefer a polished and professional look. A skilled designer can bring your vision to life and ensure that your cover art stands out in the competitive podcasting landscape.

## Examples of Effective Cover Art

Explore examples of effective cover art from successful podcasts within your niche or genre to gain inspiration and insights into design trends, styles, and techniques. Analyze what makes these cover art designs compelling and consider how you can apply similar principles to your own cover art to enhance its visual appeal and effectiveness.

Creating eye-catching cover art is an essential aspect of podcasting that can significantly impact your podcast's visibility, attract new listeners, and reinforce your brand identity. By understanding the importance of cover art, incorporating key design elements, following best practices, and seeking professional assistance when needed, you can design compelling cover art that captivates audiences and sets your podcast apart in the competitive podcasting landscape.

# 6.3 Crafting Captivating Episode Titles and Descriptions

———

Crafting captivating episode titles and descriptions is essential for attracting listeners, generating interest in your podcast episodes, and increasing overall engagement. This section explores the importance of compelling titles and descriptions, key elements to consider, and strategies for crafting them effectively.

## 6.3.1 Importance of Compelling Titles and Descriptions

COMPELLING TITLES AND descriptions serve as the first point of contact between your podcast and potential listeners. They provide a glimpse into the content of your episodes, enticing listeners to click and listen. Here's why they matter:

> **Attracting Attention:** In a sea of podcasts, a catchy title and description can help your episodes stand out and grab the attention of potential listeners browsing through podcast directories or platforms.

> **Generating Interest:** A well-crafted title and description should pique curiosity and generate interest in the episode's content. It should compel listeners to want to learn more and ultimately hit the play button.

> **Improving Discoverability:** Search algorithms on podcast platforms often use titles and descriptions to index and recommend content to users. Optimizing your titles and descriptions with relevant keywords can improve your podcast's discoverability.

> **Setting Expectations:** Clear and descriptive titles and descriptions help set expectations for listeners regarding the topic,

format, and tone of the episode. This transparency can lead to higher listener satisfaction and retention.

## 6.3.2 Key Elements to Consider

WHEN CRAFTING EPISODE titles and descriptions, several key elements should be taken into account to maximize their effectiveness:

### Clarity and Conciseness

Titles should be clear, concise, and to the point, providing a snapshot of the episode's main topic or theme. Avoid using overly cryptic or vague titles that may confuse potential listeners.

### Keyword Optimization

Incorporating relevant keywords related to your episode's content can improve its visibility in search results. Conduct keyword research to identify terms that your target audience is likely to search for and integrate them naturally into your titles and descriptions.

### Compelling Hooks

Start your descriptions with a compelling hook or teaser that captures the essence of the episode and entices listeners to continue reading. Pose a question, share an intriguing fact, or highlight a compelling story to draw readers in.

### Unique Selling Proposition (USP)

Highlight what makes your episode unique and why listeners should tune in. Whether it's exclusive insights, expert interviews, or engaging storytelling, emphasize the value proposition that sets your episode apart from others in the same niche.

### Call to Action (CTA)

Include a clear call to action at the end of your description to encourage listeners to take the next step, whether it's subscribing to your podcast, leaving a review, or visiting your website for additional resources.

### 6.3.3 Strategies for Crafting Effective Titles and Descriptions

CRAFTING EFFECTIVE titles and descriptions requires a blend of creativity, strategic thinking, and an understanding of your target audience. Here are some strategies to help you create compelling titles and descriptions:

**A/B Testing**

Experiment with different title formats, keywords, and descriptions to see which ones resonate best with your audience. A/B testing can help you identify the most effective combinations and optimize your titles and descriptions for maximum impact.

**Audience Persona Research**

Understand your target audience's preferences, pain points, and interests to tailor your titles and descriptions to their needs. Use language and messaging that resonates with your audience and speaks directly to their motivations.

**Storytelling Techniques**

Incorporate storytelling elements into your titles and descriptions to create intrigue and emotional resonance. Use vivid imagery, compelling narratives, and relatable anecdotes to captivate listeners and draw them into your episode's story.

**Consistency and Branding**

Maintain consistency in your title formatting and branding across all episodes to establish a recognizable identity for your podcast. Consistent branding builds trust with listeners and reinforces your podcast's unique voice and style.

**Feedback and Iteration**

Solicit feedback from your audience and analyze performance metrics to gauge the effectiveness of your titles and descriptions. Iterate based on feedback and insights, continuously refining your approach to better serve your audience's needs.

Crafting captivating episode titles and descriptions is an ongoing process that requires creativity, experimentation, and a deep understanding of your audience. By optimizing your titles and descriptions to attract attention, generate interest, and set clear expectations, you can effectively engage your audience and drive listenership to your podcast episodes.

# 6.4 Uploading and Publishing Episodes

Uploading and publishing episodes is the final step in the podcast production process before they become available to your audience. This section outlines the essential steps and considerations involved in uploading and publishing episodes effectively.

## 6.4.1 Preparing Your Episode Files

BEFORE UPLOADING YOUR episode, ensure that your audio files are properly formatted and edited. Follow these steps to prepare your episode files:

### File Format

Save your episodes in a compatible audio file format, such as MP3 or WAV, to ensure broad compatibility across podcast platforms.

### Audio Quality

Check the audio quality of your files to ensure they meet your podcast's standards. Remove any background noise, adjust volume levels, and apply any necessary enhancements to optimize sound quality.

### Metadata

Embed metadata, including episode title, episode number, podcast title, episode description, and any relevant tags or keywords, directly into your audio files. This metadata will be visible to listeners and helps with searchability.

### ID3 Tags

Use ID3 tags to add additional information to your audio files, such as artwork, artist name, album title, and genre. This metadata provides additional context and enhances the listener experience.

## 6.4.2 Selecting a Podcast Hosting Platform

CHOOSE A PODCAST HOSTING platform that aligns with your needs and budget. Consider factors such as storage space, bandwidth limits, analytics features, monetization options, and ease of use. Popular podcast hosting platforms include:

**Libsyn**

Known for its reliability and comprehensive analytics features, Libsyn offers various hosting plans to accommodate podcasts of all sizes.

**Podbean**

Podbean provides user-friendly hosting solutions with unlimited storage, customizable websites, and built-in monetization tools.

**Spotify for Podcasters**

Spotify for Podcasters f.k.a Anchor is a free hosting platform that offers intuitive podcast creation tools, distribution to all major platforms, and monetization options through sponsorships.

**Buzzsprout**

With its user-friendly interface and robust analytics, Buzzsprout makes it easy to upload, publish, and promote your podcast episodes.

## 6.4.3 Uploading Your Episodes

ONCE YOU'VE SELECTED a hosting platform, follow these steps to upload your episodes:

☐ **Create an Account:** Sign up for an account on your chosen hosting platform and complete the necessary setup steps, such as providing podcast details and linking your RSS feed.

☐ **Upload Episode Files:** Use the platform's dashboard or uploading tool to upload your prepared episode files. Ensure that you follow any file size or format requirements specified by the platform.

☐ **Add Episode Details:** Enter episode details such as title, description, episode number, release date, and any relevant tags or keywords. This information will be used to populate your podcast's RSS feed and metadata.

☐ **Set Episode Settings:** Configure episode settings, such as visibility (public or private), publishing schedule (immediate or scheduled), and any additional options provided by the hosting platform.

## 6.4.4 Publishing Your Episodes

AFTER UPLOADING YOUR episodes, it's time to publish them and make them available to your audience:

- **Review Episode Details:** Double-check the accuracy of episode details, including titles, descriptions, and release dates, before publishing. Ensure that all information is clear, concise, and free of errors.

- **Preview Episodes:** Use the platform's preview or playback feature to listen to each episode and verify audio quality, formatting, and any embedded metadata.

- **Publish Episodes:** Once you're satisfied with the episode details and quality, publish your episodes to make them live on your podcast hosting platform. Depending on your settings, episodes may be immediately available or scheduled for release at a later date.

# 6.5 Submitting to Podcast Directories

Submitting your podcast to directories is essential for expanding your audience reach and increasing discoverability. This section details the process of submitting your podcast to popular directories and maximizing your visibility.

## 6.5.1 Understanding Podcast Directories

PODCAST DIRECTORIES are online platforms that host and distribute podcasts to listeners. They serve as centralized hubs where users can discover, subscribe to, and listen to podcasts across various genres and categories. Some of the most popular podcast directories include:

**Apple Podcasts**

As one of the largest podcast directories, Apple Podcasts offers a vast library of podcasts across all genres. It is widely used by iOS users and provides valuable exposure to a global audience.

**Spotify**

Spotify has emerged as a major player in the podcasting space, with millions of active users worldwide. Its podcast directory features a diverse range of shows and offers personalized recommendations to listeners.

**YouTube**

Consider uploading your episode to YouTube as audio only, or if you have recorded video, this is a good option to connect with your audience through the podcast ability on the YouTube platform.

**TuneIn**

TuneIn offers a wide selection of podcasts, radio stations, and live streams to its users. Submitting your podcast to TuneIn can increase its exposure to a diverse audience of listeners.

## 6.5.2 Preparing Your Podcast for Submission

BEFORE SUBMITTING YOUR podcast to directories, ensure that it meets the platform's requirements and guidelines. Follow these steps to prepare your podcast for submission:

❖ **Review Submission Guidelines:** Familiarize yourself with the submission guidelines and requirements of each directory. Pay attention to specifications such as file format, episode length, artwork dimensions, and content policies.

❖ **Ensure Compliance:** Ensure that your podcast complies with copyright laws and regulations. Obtain necessary licenses for any copyrighted material used in your episodes, such as music, clips, or interviews.

❖ **Create High-Quality Assets:** Prepare high-quality assets for your podcast, including professional artwork, engaging episode titles, and descriptive episode descriptions. These assets play a crucial role in attracting listeners and increasing discoverability.

❖ **Generate RSS Feed:** Generate an RSS feed for your podcast using a hosting platform or podcasting service. The RSS feed contains metadata and episode information that directories use to populate your podcast listing.

## 6.5.3 Submitting to Podcast Directories

ONCE YOUR PODCAST IS prepared, follow these steps to submit it to podcast directories:

**Apple Podcasts:** Submit your podcast to Apple Podcasts through Apple's Podcasts Connect platform. Create an account, provide your podcast details and RSS feed, and await approval from Apple.

**Spotify:** Submit your podcast to Spotify using the Spotify for Podcasters platform. Sign up for an account, claim your podcast, and submit your RSS feed for review.

**TuneIn:** Submit your podcast to TuneIn by filling out the TuneIn submission form with your podcast details and RSS feed URL. TuneIn will review your submission and add your podcast to its directory.

## 6.5.4 Optimizing Your Podcast Listing

AFTER SUBMITTING YOUR podcast, optimize its listing on each directory to maximize visibility and attract listeners:

### Optimize Metadata

Review and optimize your podcast metadata, including titles, descriptions, and tags, to improve searchability and relevance.

### Update Artwork

Keep your podcast artwork up to date and visually appealing to attract potential listeners browsing the directory.

### Encourage Reviews and Ratings

Encourage listeners to leave reviews and ratings for your podcast on directories like Apple Podcasts and Stitcher. Positive reviews can enhance credibility and attract new listeners.

### Promote Your Listing

Promote your podcast listing on social media, your website, and other marketing channels to drive traffic and increase subscriptions.

### 6.5.5 Monitoring and Analyzing Performance

ONCE YOUR PODCAST IS listed on directories, monitor its performance and analyze listener data to gain insights and improve your podcast:

❖ **Track Downloads and Subscriptions:** Monitor download metrics and subscription trends to gauge the popularity and growth

❖ **Promote Episodes:** After publishing, promote your episodes across your social media channels, website, email newsletters, and other marketing channels to maximize visibility and engagement.

❖ **Monitoring Performance:** Track the performance of your episodes using the analytics tools provided by your hosting platform. Monitor metrics such as downloads, listener demographics, engagement, and retention to gain insights into your audience and improve future episodes.

Uploading and publishing episodes is a crucial step in the podcast production process. By properly preparing your episode files, selecting a suitable hosting platform, uploading episodes accurately, and monitoring performance, you can effectively share your podcast with the world and grow your audience.

# Chapter 7: Growing Your Audience

# 7.1 Effective Marketing Strategies

———

Growing your podcast audience requires strategic marketing efforts to increase visibility, attract new listeners, and retain existing ones. This section explores various marketing strategies and tactics to help you reach your audience growth goals.

## 7.1.1 Define Your Target Audience

BEFORE IMPLEMENTING marketing strategies, it's essential to clearly define your target audience. Identify demographics, interests, and preferences of your ideal listeners to tailor your marketing messages effectively.

## 7.1.2 Develop a Brand Identity

CREATE A STRONG BRAND identity for your podcast to stand out in a crowded market. Develop a unique logo, color scheme, and tone of voice that reflects your podcast's personality and resonates with your target audience.

## 7.1.3 Leverage Social Media Platforms

UTILIZE SOCIAL MEDIA platforms to promote your podcast and engage with your audience. Share engaging content, behind-the-scenes insights, and episode highlights on platforms like Twitter, Facebook, Instagram, and LinkedIn.

**Create Shareable Content:** Craft compelling social media posts, graphics, and videos that encourage your audience to share your content with their networks, expanding your reach organically.

**Engage with Your Audience:** Foster meaningful interactions with your audience by responding to comments, messages, and mentions promptly. Encourage conversation, feedback, and user-generated content to build a community around your podcast.

### 7.1.4 Utilize Email Marketing

EMAIL MARKETING IS an effective way to communicate directly with your audience and promote your podcast. Build an email list of subscribers interested in your content and send regular newsletters, episode updates, and exclusive content to keep them engaged.

**Offer Incentives:** Encourage listeners to subscribe to your email list by offering incentives such as bonus episodes, exclusive content, or downloadable resources related to your podcast niche.

**Personalize Your Communication:** Segment your email list based on subscriber preferences and behavior to deliver personalized content and offers that resonate with each segment.

### 7.1.5 Collaborate with Influencers and Guests

COLLABORATE WITH INFLUENCERS, industry experts, and other podcasters to expand your reach and tap into their existing audience. Guest appearances, cross-promotions, and interviews can introduce your podcast to new listeners and enhance your credibility.

**Identify Potential Collaborators:** Research and identify influencers, thought leaders, and podcasters in your niche who align with your podcast's values and audience demographics.

**Reach Out with Value Proposition:** Craft personalized outreach messages that highlight the mutual benefits of collaboration, such as exposure to each other's audiences, shared expertise, and cross-promotion opportunities.

### 7.1.6 Implement Search Engine Optimization (SEO)

OPTIMIZE YOUR PODCAST website, episode pages, and show notes for search engines to improve discoverability and attract organic traffic. Use relevant keywords, meta tags, and descriptive titles to rank higher in search engine results pages (SERPs).

**Keyword Research:** Conduct keyword research to identify popular search terms and phrases related to your podcast niche. Incorporate these keywords naturally into your content to increase visibility.

**Optimize Metadata:** Optimize metadata such as episode titles, descriptions, and tags with relevant keywords to improve indexing and ranking on podcast directories and search engines.

## 7.1.7 Engage with Online Communities and Forums

PARTICIPATE IN ONLINE communities, forums, and discussion groups relevant to your podcast niche to connect with potential listeners and establish your expertise. Share valuable insights, answer questions, and promote your podcast subtly within community guidelines.

**Provide Value:** Focus on providing value to community members by offering helpful advice, resources, and recommendations related to your podcast topic. Avoid overt self-promotion to maintain credibility and respect within the community.

**Network and Build Relationships:** Build genuine relationships with community members, moderators, and influencers by engaging authentically and contributing meaningfully to discussions. Networking can lead to opportunities for collaboration, guest appearances, and word-of-mouth promotion.

## 7.1.8 Analyze and Iterate

MONITOR THE PERFORMANCE of your marketing strategies and campaigns using analytics tools to track key metrics such as website traffic, social media engagement, email open rates, and conversion rates. Use data-driven insights to refine your approach, experiment with new tactics, and optimize your audience growth efforts over time.

❖ **Set Measurable Goals:** Establish clear, measurable goals for your marketing efforts, such as increasing website traffic, growing your email list, or boosting podcast downloads. Track progress regularly and adjust your strategies as needed to achieve your objectives.

❖ **A/B Testing:** Conduct A/B tests on different marketing channels, messaging, and creative elements to identify what resonates most with your audience and drives the highest results. Use test results to inform future marketing decisions and optimizations.

❖ **Stay Agile:** Stay agile and adaptable in your marketing approach, continuously learning from successes and failures, and adapting strategies based on changing audience preferences, industry trends, and platform algorithms. Flexibility is key to staying ahead in a dynamic digital landscape.

By implementing these effective marketing strategies, you can attract, engage, and retain a loyal audience for your podcast, driving sustainable growth and success in the long term.

# 7.2 Leveraging Social Media

———

Social media platforms offer powerful tools for promoting your podcast, engaging with your audience, and expanding your reach. This section explores various strategies for leveraging social media effectively to grow your podcast audience.

## 7.2.1 Choosing the Right Platforms

SELECTING THE MOST suitable social media platforms for promoting your podcast is essential for reaching your target audience effectively. Consider factors such as demographics, content format, and engagement levels when choosing platforms. Some popular social media platforms for podcast promotion include:

**Facebook**

With billions of users worldwide, Facebook provides a vast audience reach. Create a dedicated Facebook page for your podcast to share episodes, engage with followers, and join relevant groups and communities.

**Twitter**

Twitter is a fast-paced platform ideal for sharing real-time updates, engaging in conversations, and connecting with influencers and fellow podcasters. Use hashtags, mentions, and multimedia content to amplify your podcast's visibility.

**Instagram**

Instagram's visual nature makes it ideal for showcasing behind-the-scenes content, episode highlights, and user-generated content. Leverage features like Stories, IGTV, and Reels to engage your audience and drive traffic to your podcast.

**LinkedIn**

LinkedIn is a valuable platform for networking, professional branding, and sharing industry insights. Utilize LinkedIn articles, posts, and groups to establish thought leadership in your podcast niche and connect with professionals interested in your content.

### YouTube

YouTube offers a platform for hosting video podcasts, creating promotional trailers, and repurposing audio content into visually engaging videos. Leverage YouTube's search engine optimization (SEO) features to increase discoverability and attract new listeners.

### TikTok

TikTok's short-form video format is ideal for quick, engaging content that captures attention. Use trending sounds, challenges, and bite-sized clips from your podcast to increase visibility. TikTok's algorithm favors content that resonates, making it a powerful tool for reaching new audiences quickly.

## 7.2.2 Creating Compelling Content

EFFECTIVE SOCIAL MEDIA marketing relies on creating compelling and engaging content that resonates with your audience. Tailor your content to each platform's unique features and audience preferences. Consider the following strategies:

☐ **Visual Assets:** Incorporate eye-catching visuals, such as custom graphics, images, and videos, to enhance the appeal of your social media posts. Use tools like Canva or Adobe Spark to create professional-looking visuals that reflect your podcast brand.

☐ **Teasers and Previews:** Share teaser clips, snippets, or highlights from upcoming episodes to generate anticipation and excitement among your audience. Teasers provide a preview of your podcast content and entice listeners to tune in for the full episode.

☐ **Behind-the-Scenes Content: Offer** behind-the-scenes glimpses into your podcasting process, including recording sessions, guest interviews, and production workflows. Authentic behind-the-scenes content humanizes your brand and fosters a deeper connection with your audience.

☐ **Interactive Polls and Q&A Sessions:** Encourage audience engagement by hosting interactive polls, Q&A sessions, or live streams on social media. Invite listeners to participate, share their thoughts, and ask questions related to your podcast topics.

## 7.2.3 Engaging with Your Audience

BUILDING MEANINGFUL connections with your audience is crucial for fostering loyalty and driving engagement on social media. Implement the following strategies to engage with your audience effectively:

### Responding to Comments and Messages

Actively monitor comments, messages, and mentions on your social media profiles, and respond promptly to listener inquiries, feedback, and interactions. Engaging in two-way conversations demonstrates your commitment to audience engagement.

### Hosting Contests and Giveaways

Organize contests, giveaways, or challenges to incentivize audience participation and reward loyal listeners. Offer podcast merchandise, exclusive content, or promotional discounts as prizes to encourage participation and increase brand awareness.

### User-Generated Content Campaigns

Encourage your audience to create and share user-generated content related to your podcast, such as fan art, testimonials, or podcast recommendations. Highlight user-generated content on your social media channels to showcase your community's creativity and enthusiasm.

## Collaborating with Influencers and Partners

Collaborate with influencers, industry experts, or fellow podcasters to expand your reach and tap into new audience segments. Partnering with influencers for guest appearances, cross-promotions, or sponsored content can introduce your podcast to their followers and enhance credibility.

# 7.2.4 Analyzing Performance and Optimization

MONITOR THE PERFORMANCE of your social media marketing efforts and continuously optimize your strategies to maximize effectiveness. Use social media analytics tools to track key metrics, identify trends, and gain insights into audience behavior. Consider the following optimization techniques:

## Tracking Key Metrics

Monitor metrics such as engagement rate, reach, impressions, and click-through rate (CTR) to evaluate the effectiveness of your social media campaigns. Identify top-performing content, optimal posting times, and audience demographics to inform future strategies.

## A/B Testing

Experiment with different content formats, messaging styles, and posting schedules through A/B testing. Compare the performance of variations to determine the most effective approaches for engaging your audience and driving conversions.

## Content Calendar Planning

Develop a content calendar outlining your social media posting schedule, content themes, and promotional campaigns. Plan ahead for upcoming episodes, events, or seasonal trends to maintain consistency and relevance in your social media content.

## Iterative Improvement

Continuously iterate and refine your social media marketing strategies based on performance data and audience feedback. Adapt to changing trends, algorithm updates, and audience preferences to stay relevant and effective in reaching your podcasting goals.

By leveraging social media effectively, you can amplify your podcast's visibility, foster community engagement, and ultimately grow your audience organically. Experiment with different platforms, content formats, and engagement strategies to find what resonates best with your target audience and drives meaningful results.

# 7.3 Collaborating with Other Podcasters

———

Collaborating with other podcasters offers valuable opportunities to expand your audience, share expertise, and cross-promote content. This section explores effective strategies for collaborating with fellow podcasters to mutual benefit.

## 7.3.1 Identifying Potential Collaborators

BEFORE REACHING OUT to other podcasters, it's essential to identify potential collaborators whose content aligns with your podcast's niche, audience, and values. Consider the following factors when evaluating potential collaborators:

**Relevance**

Look for podcasters whose content complements yours or addresses similar topics of interest to your audience. Collaborating with relevant podcasters increases the likelihood of attracting listeners who share common interests.

**Audience Size and Engagement**

Assess the size and engagement level of potential collaborators' audiences to gauge the potential reach and impact of collaboration efforts. While larger audiences offer broader exposure, smaller audiences with high engagement rates may yield more targeted results.

**Compatibility**

Evaluate the compatibility of potential collaborators in terms of communication style, values, and professionalism. Establishing rapport and mutual respect with collaborators is essential for fostering productive and harmonious partnerships.

## 7.3.2 Approaching Collaborators

WHEN REACHING OUT TO potential collaborators, it's crucial to approach them respectfully, clearly articulate your collaboration proposal, and highlight the mutual benefits. Consider the following tips for initiating collaboration:

**Personalized Outreach**

Tailor your outreach messages to each potential collaborator, demonstrating genuine interest in their work and explaining how collaboration aligns with their goals and interests.

**Value Proposition**

Clearly articulate the value proposition of collaboration, emphasizing how it benefits both parties in terms of audience growth, content quality, and mutual support.

**Collaboration Ideas**

Propose specific collaboration ideas or formats, such as guest appearances, co-hosted episodes, interview swaps, or joint promotional campaigns. Provide details on how collaboration would enhance both podcasts and appeal to shared audiences.

## 7.3.3 Coordinating Collaboration Efforts

ONCE COLLABORATION opportunities are identified and agreed upon, it's essential to coordinate efforts effectively to ensure smooth execution and maximize impact. Consider the following aspects of collaboration coordination:

**Clear Communication**

Maintain open and transparent communication with collaborators throughout the collaboration process. Establish clear timelines, responsibilities, and expectations to avoid misunderstandings or conflicts.

**Content Planning**

Collaborate with your partners to plan and coordinate content creation, including episode topics, formats, and release schedules. Ensure that collaborative content aligns with both podcasts' branding and audience preferences.

**Promotion Strategy**

Develop a comprehensive promotion strategy to amplify collaborative content across both podcasts' platforms and social media channels. Coordinate promotional efforts, such as cross-promotional trailers, social media posts, and newsletter mentions, to maximize reach and engagement.

## 7.3.4 Maximizing Collaboration Impact

TO MAXIMIZE THE IMPACT of collaboration efforts, focus on delivering high-quality content, fostering genuine connections with collaborators and their audiences, and leveraging cross-promotional opportunities effectively. Consider the following strategies:

**Value-Driven Content**

Prioritize delivering value to both podcasts' audiences through informative, entertaining, and engaging content. Emphasize authenticity, expertise, and unique perspectives to captivate listeners and encourage long-term engagement.

**Audience Engagement**

Actively engage with collaborators and their audiences before, during, and after collaboration efforts. Respond to listener feedback, participate in discussions, and encourage cross-pollination of audiences to foster community engagement and loyalty.

**Long-Term Relationships**

Cultivate long-term relationships with collaborators based on trust, reciprocity, and mutual support. Explore ongoing collaboration opportunities, such as recurring guest appearances, joint projects, or co-branded initiatives, to maintain momentum and deepen connections over time.

**Performance Evaluation**

Continuously evaluate the performance of collaboration efforts based on key metrics such as audience growth, engagement, and feedback. Identify successful strategies and areas for improvement to refine future collaboration initiatives and optimize results.

By collaborating with other podcasters strategically and authentically, you can leverage each other's strengths, reach new audiences, and foster a sense of community within the podcasting ecosystem. Approach collaboration opportunities with professionalism, creativity, and a genuine desire to create value for both parties and their audiences.

# 7.4 Encouraging Listener Engagement

═══

Listener engagement is vital for building a loyal audience, fostering community, and driving podcast growth. This section delves into effective strategies for encouraging listener engagement and fostering meaningful interactions with your audience.

## 7.4.1 Creating Interactive Content

INTERACTIVE CONTENT encourages active participation from listeners, fostering a sense of involvement and investment in your podcast. Consider implementing the following strategies to create interactive content:

**Audience Q&A Sessions**

Host dedicated Q&A episodes or segments where listeners can submit questions, comments, or topic suggestions. Encourage audience participation by inviting them to engage with your content and contribute to future episodes.

**Polls and Surveys**

Conduct polls and surveys to gather feedback from your audience and involve them in decision-making processes. Use survey responses to tailor content to listeners' preferences, interests, and needs, fostering a sense of ownership and relevance.

**Interactive Challenges or Contests**

Organize interactive challenges, contests, or giveaways that encourage listeners to participate and interact with your podcast. Offer incentives such as exclusive content, merchandise, or recognition to incentivize engagement and reward active listeners.

## 7.4.2 Fostering Community Engagement

BUILDING A SENSE OF community around your podcast strengthens listener loyalty, fosters peer-to-peer connections, and creates a supportive network of fans. Explore the following strategies to foster community engagement:

### Social Media Groups or Forums

Create dedicated social media groups, forums, or online communities where listeners can connect, share ideas, and discuss podcast-related topics. Actively participate in these communities to facilitate discussions, answer questions, and nurture relationships with your audience.

### Live Events and Meetups

Organize live events, meetups, or virtual gatherings to bring listeners together in person or online. Provide opportunities for listeners to interact with you and fellow fans, fostering a sense of belonging and camaraderie within the community.

### Collaborative Projects

Collaborate with your audience on collaborative projects, such as crowd-sourced episodes, listener-generated content, or community-driven initiatives. Empower listeners to contribute their creativity, expertise, and perspectives to enrich the podcasting experience for everyone involved.

## 7.4.3 Leveraging Call-to-Action (CTA) Strategies

STRATEGIC USE OF CALL-to-action (CTA) prompts encourages listeners to take specific actions, such as subscribing, sharing, or leaving reviews, to deepen engagement and support podcast growth. Implement the following CTA strategies effectively:

☐ **Subscription and Review Requests:** Encourage listeners to subscribe to your podcast and leave reviews or ratings on podcast platforms. Include subscription and review requests in your episodes, show notes, and social media posts to streamline the process and maximize response rates.

☐ **Social Sharing and Referrals:** Prompt listeners to share episodes with their networks and refer friends or colleagues to your podcast. Provide easy-to-share links, social media buttons, and referral incentives to facilitate sharing and expand your podcast's reach through word-of-mouth marketing.

☐ **Engagement Prompts:** Prompt listeners to engage with your content by posing questions, soliciting feedback, or inviting participation in specific activities. Use clear and compelling language to motivate action and create opportunities for meaningful interaction with your audience.

## 7.4.4 Monitoring and Responding to Listener Feedback

REGULARLY MONITORING listener feedback and responding promptly demonstrates attentiveness, fosters trust, and strengthens relationships with your audience. Implement the following practices to effectively manage listener feedback:

**Feedback Collection Channels**

Provide multiple channels for listeners to submit feedback, including email, social media, website forms, and voicemail. Regularly check these channels and acknowledge receipt of feedback to reassure listeners that their input is valued.

**Active Listening and Response**

Actively listen to listener feedback, paying attention to both positive comments and constructive criticism. Respond promptly and courteously to feedback, addressing questions, concerns, and suggestions with transparency and empathy.

**Feedback Integration**

Integrate listener feedback into your podcasting process by incorporating relevant suggestions, addressing common issues, and adapting content based on audience preferences. Demonstrate responsiveness to feedback to show listeners that their input directly influences the evolution of your podcast.

By implementing these strategies, you can cultivate a vibrant and engaged listener community around your podcast, fostering meaningful interactions, building loyalty, and driving sustained growth over time. Prioritize authenticity, value, and responsiveness in your engagement efforts to create lasting connections with your audience and enhance the overall podcasting experience.

# 7.5 Analyzing Podcast Analytics

Understanding podcast analytics is essential for optimizing your content strategy, refining marketing efforts, and maximizing audience engagement. This section explores various aspects of podcast analytics and provides insights into leveraging data-driven insights to grow your audience effectively.

## 7.5.1 Key Metrics and Performance Indicators

ANALYZING PODCAST ANALYTICS begins with identifying key metrics and performance indicators that provide valuable insights into audience behavior, content performance, and overall podcast growth. Some essential metrics to monitor include:

❖ **Downloads and Listens:** Track the number of downloads or listens your episodes receive over time to gauge audience reach and engagement. Analyze trends in download metrics to identify popular episodes, seasonal patterns, and areas for improvement.

❖ **Audience Demographics:** Gain insights into your audience demographics, including age, gender, location, and interests, to better understand your target audience and tailor content to their preferences and needs.

❖ **Engagement Metrics:** Monitor engagement metrics such as play duration, completion rates, and listener retention to assess audience engagement levels and identify content areas that resonate most with your audience.

❖ **Subscriber Growth:** Track subscriber growth and retention rates to evaluate the effectiveness of your marketing efforts, audience acquisition strategies, and content initiatives in driving sustained audience growth.

❖ **Listener Feedback and Reviews:** Monitor listener feedback, reviews, and ratings to gauge audience satisfaction, sentiment, and perception of your podcast. Use feedback insights to identify areas for improvement and enhance the overall listener experience.

## 7.5.2 Tools and Platforms for Podcast Analytics

UTILIZE A VARIETY OF tools and platforms to collect, analyze, and interpret podcast analytics effectively. Some popular podcast analytics tools and platforms include:

### Podcast Hosting Platforms

Many podcast hosting platforms offer built-in analytics dashboards that provide insights into download statistics, audience demographics, engagement metrics, and listener feedback.

### Third-Party Analytics Tools

Explore third-party analytics tools and services specifically designed for podcasters, offering advanced analytics features, customizable reports, and actionable insights to optimize podcast performance.

### Social Media Analytics

Leverage social media analytics tools to track audience engagement, referral traffic, and content performance across social media platforms. Analyze social media metrics to assess the impact of social media marketing efforts on podcast growth.

### Website Analytics

Integrate website analytics tools such as Google Analytics to track website traffic, user behavior, and conversion metrics. Monitor website analytics to understand how website visitors discover and engage with your podcast content.

## 7.5.3 Interpreting and Applying Analytics Insights

INTERPRETING PODCAST analytics insights requires a nuanced understanding of audience behavior, content performance, and industry trends. Apply the following strategies to interpret and apply analytics insights effectively:

**Performance Benchmarking**

Compare your podcast analytics data against industry benchmarks, competitors' metrics, and past performance to identify areas of strength, weakness, and opportunity for improvement.

**Iterative Experimentation**

Conduct iterative experimentation by testing different content formats, marketing strategies, and audience engagement tactics based on analytics insights. Measure the impact of changes on key metrics and adjust strategies accordingly to optimize podcast performance.

**Data-Driven Decision-Making**

Make data-driven decisions by prioritizing analytics insights in content planning, marketing campaigns, and audience engagement initiatives. Use analytics data to inform content strategy, audience targeting, and resource allocation to maximize podcast growth and impact.

**Continuous Monitoring and Optimization**

Continuously monitor podcast analytics data and iterate on strategies to adapt to changing audience preferences, industry trends, and market dynamics. Stay agile and responsive to analytics insights to maintain momentum and drive sustained audience growth.

By leveraging podcast analytics effectively, you can gain valuable insights into audience behavior, content performance, and marketing effectiveness, enabling you to refine your strategies, enhance audience engagement, and achieve your podcasting goals effectively. Prioritize data-driven decision-making, continuous optimization, and strategic experimentation to unlock the full potential of podcast analytics in growing your audience and maximizing podcast impact.

# Chapter 8: Monetizing Your Podcast

Monetizing your podcast is a crucial step towards turning your passion project into a sustainable source of income. This chapter delves into various monetization models and strategies to help you generate revenue from your podcasting efforts effectively.

# 8.1 Exploring Different Monetization Models

M onetizing your podcast involves exploring different revenue streams and monetization models tailored to your audience, content, and goals. Understanding the various monetization models available can help you develop a comprehensive monetization strategy that aligns with your podcasting objectives. Below are some common monetization models for podcasts:

## 8.1.1 Advertising and Sponsorships

ADVERTISING AND SPONSORSHIPS are one of the most common monetization models for podcasts. Podcasters can collaborate with advertisers and sponsors to feature sponsored content, product placements, or ad spots within their episodes. Advertising revenue can be generated through various methods, including:

**Dynamic Ad Insertion**

Incorporate dynamically inserted ads into your podcast episodes, allowing advertisers to target specific audiences based on demographics, interests, and listening behavior.

**Host-Read Ads**

Host-read ads are personalized endorsements delivered by the podcast host, often integrated seamlessly into the episode content. Host-read ads tend to be more engaging and effective in driving conversions.

**Affiliate Marketing**

Partner with affiliate programs and promote products or services relevant to your audience. Earn commissions for every referral or sale generated through your affiliate links.

## 8.1.2 Listener Support and Donations

LISTENER SUPPORT AND donations provide an alternative revenue stream for podcasters, allowing them to monetize their content directly through listener contributions. Podcasters can leverage various platforms and methods to facilitate listener support, including:

**Patreon**

Create a Patreon account to offer exclusive content, perks, and benefits to patrons in exchange for recurring monthly donations. Patreon provides a platform for building a community around your podcast and rewarding loyal supporters.

**Tip Jars and Donation Platforms**

Integrate tip jars or donation buttons on your podcast website or episode descriptions, allowing listeners to contribute voluntary donations to support your podcasting efforts.

**Merchandise Sales**

Develop and sell branded merchandise such as apparel, accessories, or digital products related to your podcast. Merchandise sales can serve as an additional revenue stream while also strengthening your brand identity and fostering listener engagement.

## 8.1.3 Premium Content and Subscription Models

PREMIUM CONTENT AND subscription models offer listeners exclusive access to premium or bonus content in exchange for a subscription fee. Podcasters can monetize their content through subscription-based platforms or premium membership programs, including:

☑ **Subscription-Based Platforms:** Partner with subscription-based podcasting platforms that offer premium content behind a paywall or subscription fee. Provide subscribers with ad-free episodes, bonus episodes, early access, or exclusive content.

☑ **Membership Programs:** Create a membership program or premium podcasting network where subscribers gain access to exclusive perks, community forums, live events, and premium content libraries. Offer tiered membership options with varying levels of benefits and pricing.

☑ **Pay-Per-Listen or Paywalled Episodes:** Monetize individual episodes or series by gating access to premium content behind a pay-per-listen or paywall model. Listeners can purchase access to specific episodes or series, unlocking premium content for a one-time fee.

## 8.1.4 Product Sales and E-Commerce

PRODUCT SALES AND E-commerce present opportunities for podcasters to monetize their audience by selling physical or digital products related to their podcast niche. Podcasters can monetize their audience through various e-commerce strategies, including:

> **Digital Products:** Create and sell digital products such as e-books, online courses, exclusive content bundles, or premium subscriptions. Leverage your expertise and unique insights to develop valuable digital products tailored to your audience's interests and needs.

> **Physical Merchandise:** Design and sell physical merchandise such as branded merchandise, apparel, accessories, or merchandise bundles. Partner with print-on-demand services or fulfillment companies to handle inventory, production, and shipping logistics.

> **Affiliate Partnerships:** Partner with e-commerce platforms, brands, or retailers as affiliate partners to promote relevant products or services to your audience. Earn commissions for every sale or referral generated through your affiliate links, leveraging your podcast's influence to drive conversions.

> **Drop-shipping:** Explore drop-shipping as a low-risk e-commerce model for selling physical products without the need for inventory management or upfront capital investment. Partner with drop-shipping suppliers to fulfill orders directly to customers, earning a profit margin on each sale.

## 8.1.5 Live Events and Sponsorships

LIVE EVENTS AND SPONSORSHIPS offer opportunities for podcasters to monetize their audience through live performances, speaking engagements, or sponsored events. Podcasters can collaborate with event organizers, sponsors, or venues to monetize live events through:

### Live Shows and Performances

Organize live podcast recordings, live-streamed events, or live performances for your audience, charging admission fees or ticket prices for attendance. Monetize live events through ticket sales, merchandise sales, sponsorships, or VIP packages.

### Speaking Engagements and Workshops

Book speaking engagements, workshops, or educational sessions related to your podcast niche. Monetize speaking engagements through speaker fees, event sponsorships, or product sales during the event.

### Sponsored Events and Partnerships

Partner with brands, sponsors, or event organizers to host sponsored events, product launches, or branded experiences. Monetize sponsored events through sponsorship deals, brand partnerships, or product placements.

### Community Meetups and Fan Engagement

Host community meetups, fan conventions, or fan engagement events to connect with your audience and foster community engagement. Monetize community events through ticket sales, merchandise sales, sponsorships, or exclusive VIP experiences.

Exploring different monetization models allows podcasters to diversify their revenue streams, maximize earnings potential, and build a sustainable business around their podcasting efforts. By combining multiple monetization strategies, podcasters can create value for their audience while generating income from their content, ultimately fueling the growth and success of their podcasting endeavors.

# 8.2 Sponsorships and Advertising

Sponsorships and advertising are primary revenue streams for many podcasters, offering opportunities to collaborate with brands and advertisers to promote products or services to their audience. This section explores the intricacies of sponsorships and advertising within the podcasting landscape, covering various aspects such as finding sponsors, negotiating deals, creating effective ad placements, and maximizing revenue potential.

## 8.2.1 Finding Sponsors

FINDING SPONSORS REQUIRES proactive outreach, networking, and establishing credibility within your niche. Here are some strategies for finding sponsors for your podcast:

❖ **Identify Potential Sponsors:** Research brands and companies that align with your podcast's niche, target audience, and values. Look for brands that offer products or services relevant to your listeners' interests and needs.

❖ **Reach Out to Prospective Sponsors:** Craft personalized sponsorship proposals or pitches highlighting the value proposition of sponsoring your podcast. Reach out to prospective sponsors via email, social media, or networking events, showcasing your podcast's reach, engagement, and demographics.

❖ **Utilize Sponsorship Marketplaces:** Explore sponsorship marketplaces and platforms that connect podcasters with advertisers and sponsors. Platforms like Podcorn, Anchor Sponsorships, and AdvertiseCast facilitate sponsorships and advertising opportunities for podcasters of all sizes.

❖ **Leverage Your Network:** Tap into your existing network and connections within your industry or niche to identify potential sponsors or referrals. Attend industry events, conferences, or networking meetups to expand your network and explore sponsorship opportunities.

## 8.2.2 Negotiating Sponsorship Deals

NEGOTIATING SPONSORSHIP deals requires effective communication, negotiation skills, and understanding your podcast's value proposition. Consider the following tips when negotiating sponsorship deals:

☑ **Know Your Worth:** Understand the value of your podcast audience, engagement metrics, and reach when negotiating sponsorship deals. Highlight your podcast's unique selling points, demographics, listener loyalty, and engagement rates to demonstrate value to potential sponsors.

☑ **Define Clear Terms:** Clearly define the terms and conditions of the sponsorship agreement, including deliverables, ad placements, sponsorship duration, pricing, payment terms, and performance metrics. Ensure both parties have a clear understanding of expectations and obligations.

☑ **Negotiate Fair Rates:** Negotiate fair and competitive rates based on industry standards, your podcast's metrics, audience size, and the scope of the sponsorship agreement. Consider factors such as CPM (cost per mille), CPA (cost per acquisition), or flat-rate sponsorship fees based on ad placements and duration.

☑ **Seek Win-Win Partnerships:** Strive to establish mutually beneficial partnerships with sponsors that align with your podcast's values, content, and audience preferences. Look for sponsors who are genuinely interested in reaching your audience and providing value to your listeners.

### 8.2.3 Creating Effective Ad Placements

CREATING EFFECTIVE ad placements involves strategically integrating sponsor messages into your podcast episodes to maximize impact and engagement. Consider the following tips for creating effective ad placements:

**Understand Your Audience**

Tailor ad placements to resonate with your audience's interests, preferences, and demographics. Consider the tone, style, and format of your podcast content when crafting ad scripts and placements to ensure alignment with your audience's expectations.

**Integrate Seamlessly**

Integrate sponsor messages seamlessly into your podcast episodes to avoid disrupting the listener experience. Incorporate sponsored content organically within your episode flow, using natural transitions and authentic endorsements to maintain listener engagement.

**Provide Value**

Ensure sponsored content provides value to your audience by featuring products, services, or offers relevant to their needs and interests. Focus on highlighting the benefits, features, and unique selling points of sponsored products or services to resonate with your audience.

**Optimize Ad Frequency**

Strike a balance between ad frequency and listener experience to avoid overwhelming or alienating your audience with excessive ads. Consider spacing out ad placements evenly throughout your episodes and limiting the number of ads per episode to maintain listener engagement.

**Track Performance**

Monitor and track the performance of sponsored content using analytics, tracking links, or promotional codes to evaluate the effectiveness of ad placements. Analyze metrics such as click-through rates, conversion rates, and listener feedback to optimize future ad placements and improve ROI for sponsors.

## 8.2.4 Maximizing Revenue Potential

MAXIMIZING REVENUE potential from sponsorships and advertising requires strategic planning, optimization, and ongoing refinement. Here are some strategies for maximizing revenue potential from sponsorships and advertising:

### Diversify Revenue Streams

Explore additional revenue streams such as affiliate marketing, listener support, merchandise sales, or premium content offerings to complement sponsorships and advertising revenue. Diversifying your revenue streams can help mitigate reliance on a single revenue source and increase overall earnings potential.

### Optimize Ad Rates

Continuously evaluate and optimize your ad rates based on audience growth, engagement metrics, and market demand. Adjust ad rates periodically to reflect changes in audience demographics, listener engagement, and industry trends, ensuring competitive pricing and maximizing revenue potential.

### Negotiate Renewals and Upsells

Proactively negotiate sponsorship renewals and upsell opportunities with existing sponsors based on campaign performance, audience growth, and listener feedback. Demonstrate the value and ROI of sponsoring your podcast to encourage long-term partnerships and upsell opportunities.

### Explore Premium Ad Inventory

Develop premium ad inventory or exclusive sponsorship packages with added value propositions such as premium placement, extended reach, or enhanced promotional opportunities. Offer premium ad inventory at premium rates to maximize revenue potential from advertisers seeking premium exposure.

### Invest in Audience Growth

Invest in audience growth strategies such as marketing, promotion, and content optimization to expand your podcast's reach and attract more sponsors and advertisers. Focus on growing your audience size, engagement metrics, and listener demographics to increase your podcast's appeal to potential sponsors.

By implementing these strategies, podcasters can effectively monetize their content through sponsorships and advertising, maximizing revenue potential and building a sustainable business around their podcasting endeavors.

# 8.3 Crowdfunding and Donations

———

Crowdfunding and donations offer podcasters alternative revenue streams by directly engaging their audience and community in supporting their content creation efforts. This section delves into the nuances of crowdfunding campaigns, donation strategies, and cultivating listener support to sustain and grow your podcasting endeavors.

## 8.3.1 Crowdfunding Platforms

CROWDFUNDING PLATFORMS provide podcasters with the infrastructure to launch fundraising campaigns, collect donations, and offer rewards to backers. Here are some popular crowdfunding platforms for podcasters:

❖ **Patreon:** Patreon enables creators to set up membership tiers, offering exclusive content, perks, and rewards to subscribers in exchange for recurring monthly payments. Podcasters can leverage Patreon to cultivate a community of loyal supporters and generate ongoing revenue.

❖ **Kickstarter:** Kickstarter allows creators to launch one-time fundraising campaigns for specific podcast projects or seasons. Creators set funding goals, offer rewards to backers, and receive funds only if the campaign reaches its funding target within a specified timeframe.

❖ **Indiegogo:** Indiegogo offers flexible crowdfunding options, allowing creators to choose between fixed or flexible funding models for their podcast projects. Creators can offer rewards, perks, and exclusive content to incentivize donations from supporters.

❖ **GoFundMe:** GoFundMe is a popular fundraising platform for personal causes, charitable endeavors, and creative projects, including podcasting. Creators can launch fundraising campaigns to cover production costs, equipment upgrades, or other podcast-related expenses.

## 8.3.2 Crafting Compelling Campaigns

CRAFTING COMPELLING crowdfunding campaigns requires strategic planning, storytelling, and engagement with your audience. Consider the following tips for launching successful crowdfunding campaigns:

★ **Set Clear Goals:** Define clear and achievable funding goals for your crowdfunding campaign, outlining how the funds will be used to support your podcasting efforts. Communicate the purpose, scope, and impact of your campaign to potential backers to inspire support.

★ **Offer Irresistible Rewards:** Offer enticing rewards, perks, and incentives to backers at different pledge levels to encourage donations. Consider offering exclusive content, merchandise, behind-the-scenes access, or personalized shoutouts to backers to enhance the value proposition of supporting your podcast.

★ **Tell Your Story:** Craft a compelling narrative and storytelling arc for your crowdfunding campaign, highlighting your podcast's journey, mission, and impact on listeners. Share personal anecdotes, success stories, and testimonials to connect with potential backers on an emotional level and inspire support for your cause.

★ **Engage Your Community:** Actively engage with your audience and community throughout the crowdfunding campaign, soliciting feedback, sharing updates, and rallying support through social media, email newsletters, and live events. Foster a sense of ownership and belonging among supporters, encouraging them to become advocates for your podcast.

★ **Express Gratitude:** Express gratitude and appreciation to your backers and supporters throughout and after the crowdfunding campaign. Acknowledge their contributions, celebrate milestones, and deliver on promised rewards to foster goodwill and long-term relationships with your supporters.

### 8.3.3 Cultivating Listener Donations

IN ADDITION TO CROWDFUNDING campaigns, podcasters can cultivate listener donations through various channels and strategies. Here are some effective approaches for encouraging listener donations:

☑ **Incorporate Call-to-Action:** Include clear and compelling calls-to-action (CTAs) in your podcast episodes, encouraging listeners to support your show through donations, subscriptions, or merchandise purchases. Place CTAs strategically at the beginning, middle, or end of episodes to maximize visibility and impact.

☑ **Create Donation Channels:** Provide multiple channels and platforms for listeners to donate or support your podcast, including direct donations via PayPal, Venmo, or Cash App, as well as cryptocurrency donations or in-app tipping features on podcast platforms.

☑ **Offer Membership Programs:** Establish membership or subscription programs for your podcast, offering exclusive content, ad-free episodes, early access, or premium perks to subscribers in exchange for recurring donations or membership fees. Develop a sense of community and belonging among members, fostering loyalty and ongoing support.

☑ **Host Fundraising Events:** Organize fundraising events, live streams, or virtual meetups for your audience, inviting listeners to contribute donations, participate in Q&A sessions, or interact with special guests. Create a sense of excitement and camaraderie around fundraising events, encouraging active participation and support from your community.

☑ **Express Appreciation:** Regularly express appreciation and gratitude to your listeners for their support, whether through shoutouts, personalized messages, or special acknowledgments in your episodes. Make donors feel valued and appreciated for their contributions, reinforcing their connection to your podcast and incentivizing continued support.

By implementing these strategies, podcasters can leverage crowdfunding and donations to generate revenue, cultivate listener support, and sustain their podcasting endeavors over the long term.

# 8.4 Merchandising and Product Sales

———

Merchandising and product sales offer podcasters an additional revenue stream by leveraging their brand, audience, and content to create and sell physical or digital products. This section explores the opportunities, strategies, and considerations for monetizing your podcast through merchandise and product sales.

## 8.4.1 Understanding Merchandising Opportunities

MERCHANDISING ENCOMPASSES a wide range of products and merchandise that podcasters can create and sell to their audience. From branded apparel and accessories to digital downloads and exclusive content, podcasters have numerous opportunities to monetize their brand and content through merchandise sales. Some popular merchandising opportunities include:

**Branded Apparel**

Create and sell branded apparel such as t-shirts, hoodies, hats, and socks featuring your podcast logo, artwork, or catchphrases. Branded apparel allows fans to show their support for your podcast while providing a tangible way to connect with your brand.

**Accessories and Collectibles**

Expand your merchandise offerings with accessories and collectibles such as mugs, stickers, pins, posters, or keychains. These items offer additional ways for fans to engage with your podcast and express their fandom.

**Digital Downloads**

Offer digital downloads of exclusive content, bonus episodes, behind-the-scenes footage, or special interviews as part of your merchandise offerings. Digital downloads provide instant gratification for fans while generating revenue without the need for physical inventory.

**Subscription Boxes**

Curate and sell subscription boxes filled with podcast-related merchandise, exclusive products, and surprise goodies for subscribers. Subscription boxes offer a recurring revenue stream and provide fans with a fun and engaging way to support your podcast.

**Event Merchandise**

Create and sell merchandise specifically for live events, meetups, or fan conventions associated with your podcast. Event merchandise such as limited-edition posters, commemorative items, or autographed memorabilia can generate excitement and anticipation among fans.

## 8.4.2 Setting Up Merchandise Sales

SETTING UP MERCHANDISE sales requires careful planning, design, production, and distribution to ensure a seamless and successful process. Consider the following steps when launching your merchandise sales:

**Design and Branding**

Develop cohesive branding and design elements for your merchandise, including your podcast logo, color scheme, typography, and artwork. Ensure that your merchandise reflects the identity and aesthetic of your podcast, resonating with your target audience.

**Product Selection**

Choose high-quality products and materials for your merchandise, considering factors such as comfort, durability, and visual appeal. Research suppliers, manufacturers, and fulfillment partners to find reliable vendors that can meet your quality standards and production needs.

**E-commerce Platform**

Select an e-commerce platform or online marketplace to host your merchandise sales. Choose a platform that offers customizable storefronts, secure payment processing, shipping integration, and inventory management features to streamline the sales process.

### Online Store Setup

Set up your online store or storefront, customizing product listings, pricing, descriptions, and images to showcase your merchandise effectively. Optimize your store layout and navigation for a seamless shopping experience, making it easy for customers to browse, select, and purchase products.

### Order Fulfillment

Establish efficient order fulfillment processes to manage inventory, process orders, pack products, and ship merchandise to customers in a timely manner. Consider outsourcing fulfillment to third-party logistics providers or fulfillment centers to streamline operations and scale your merchandise sales.

### Marketing and Promotion

Promote your merchandise through various marketing channels, including your podcast, website, social media, email newsletters, and advertising campaigns. Highlight the unique features, benefits, and value propositions of your merchandise to entice customers and drive sales.

### Customer Engagement

Engage with customers and fans through personalized interactions, social media engagement, and community-building efforts. Encourage customer reviews, feedback, and user-generated content to foster loyalty and advocacy among your audience.

## 8.4.3 Maximizing Merchandise Revenue

MAXIMIZING MERCHANDISE revenue requires ongoing promotion, innovation, and engagement with your audience. Consider the following strategies to optimize your merchandise sales and revenue:

## Seasonal Campaigns

Launch seasonal merchandise campaigns tied to holidays, special events, or podcast milestones to generate excitement and urgency among fans. Offer limited-edition products, holiday-themed items, or exclusive discounts to incentivize purchases during peak seasons.

## Cross-Promotion

Collaborate with other creators, brands, or influencers to cross-promote merchandise and expand your reach to new audiences. Partner with complementary podcasts, online communities, or niche influencers to promote each other's merchandise and leverage shared audiences.

## Bundle Deals

Create bundle deals and package offers to encourage customers to purchase multiple items or higher-value packages. Bundle related products together, offer discounted pricing, or include exclusive bonuses to increase the perceived value and incentivize larger purchases.

## Limited Editions

Release limited-edition merchandise collections or exclusive drops to create scarcity and drive demand among collectors and fans. Offer limited quantities of special items, autographed merchandise, or rare variants to create a sense of exclusivity and urgency.

## Subscriber Exclusives

Reward subscribers, patrons, or members with exclusive access to merchandise, discounts, or early releases as part of their subscription benefits. Offer special perks and incentives to incentivize ongoing support and loyalty from your most dedicated fans.

## Community Feedback

Solicit feedback and input from your audience when designing new merchandise or planning future releases. Engage with your community through polls, surveys, or focus groups to gather insights, preferences, and suggestions for merchandise designs and offerings.

By implementing these strategies, podcasters can leverage merchandise and product sales to diversify their revenue streams, engage their audience, and monetize their brand and content effectively.

# 8.5 Measuring and Maximizing Revenue

―――

Measuring and maximizing revenue is essential for podcasters looking to monetize their content effectively. In this section, we'll explore the importance of tracking revenue metrics, optimizing monetization strategies, and maximizing earnings potential.

## 8.5.1 Tracking Revenue Metrics

TO EFFECTIVELY MONETIZE your podcast, it's crucial to track key revenue metrics that provide insights into your earnings, performance, and audience engagement. Here are some essential revenue metrics to monitor:

**Total Revenue**

Track your total revenue from all monetization sources, including advertising, sponsorships, merchandise sales, donations, and subscription revenue. This metric gives you a comprehensive overview of your podcast's earning potential.

**Revenue Sources**

Break down your revenue by source to understand which monetization strategies are most effective. Monitor revenue from advertising campaigns, sponsorships, affiliate partnerships, merchandise sales, premium content subscriptions, and other revenue streams.

**CPM (Cost Per Mille)**

CPM represents the cost per thousand impressions for advertising campaigns and sponsorships. It measures the price advertisers pay for every thousand listens or downloads of their ad. Tracking CPM helps you evaluate the performance and profitability of your advertising partnerships.

**Conversion Rates**

Measure the conversion rates for various monetization strategies, such as affiliate marketing, merchandise sales, and premium subscriptions. Calculate the percentage of listeners who take desired actions, such as making a purchase or subscribing, to assess the effectiveness of your monetization efforts.

**Customer Lifetime Value (CLV)**

CLV estimates the total revenue generated by an average customer over their lifetime engagement with your podcast. Calculate CLV by multiplying the average customer value by the average customer lifespan. Tracking CLV helps you understand the long-term profitability of your audience.

**Return on Investment (ROI)**

Evaluate the ROI for different monetization initiatives to determine their profitability and effectiveness. Calculate ROI by dividing the net profit generated by an initiative by the total investment cost and expressing the result as a percentage. Assessing ROI helps you allocate resources wisely and prioritize high-impact monetization strategies.

**Subscriber Growth and Churn Rate**

Monitor subscriber growth and churn rate for premium content subscriptions or membership programs. Track the number of new subscribers gained and the rate at which subscribers cancel their memberships over time. Understanding subscriber growth and churn helps you optimize retention efforts and maximize subscription revenue.

## 8.5.2 Optimizing Monetization Strategies

ONCE YOU'VE ESTABLISHED baseline revenue metrics, focus on optimizing your monetization strategies to maximize earnings and audience engagement. Here are some strategies to consider:

**Diversify Revenue Streams**

Explore multiple monetization avenues, including advertising, sponsorships, merchandise sales, affiliate marketing, premium content subscriptions, live events, and crowdfunding. Diversifying revenue streams minimizes reliance on any single source and increases overall earning potential.

## Audience Segmentation

Segment your audience based on demographics, interests, behaviors, and purchasing patterns to tailor monetization strategies to specific audience segments. Customize advertising campaigns, merchandise offerings, and premium content to resonate with different audience segments and maximize conversion rates.

## Content Monetization

Monetize your podcast content by offering premium or exclusive episodes, bonus content, ad-free listening experiences, early access to episodes, or behind-the-scenes footage through subscription models or membership programs. Provide value-added benefits to subscribers to incentivize paid engagement and generate recurring revenue.

## Optimize Ad Placement and Frequency

Balance ad placement and frequency to maximize revenue without sacrificing listener experience. Experiment with different ad formats, placement options, and frequency caps to find the optimal balance between monetization and audience retention. Consider integrating native ads, host-read endorsements, and sponsored segments for seamless integration and higher engagement.

## Engagement Strategies

Engage with your audience through interactive features, community-building initiatives, and exclusive perks to foster deeper connections and increase loyalty. Encourage listener participation, feedback, and user-generated content to create a sense of belonging and incentivize support for your podcast.

## Continuous Experimentation

Continuously experiment with new monetization strategies, partnerships, pricing models, and promotional tactics to identify what works best for your podcast and audience. Test different approaches, analyze performance data, and iterate based on insights to optimize revenue generation over time.

### 8.5.3 Maximizing Earnings Potential

MAXIMIZING EARNINGS potential requires a proactive approach to revenue optimization, audience engagement, and business development. Here are some additional tips to help you maximize your podcast's earning potential:

**Build Strong Partnerships**

Forge strategic partnerships with advertisers, sponsors, brands, and affiliates that align with your podcast's values, niche, and audience interests. Cultivate long-term relationships based on mutual trust, transparency, and shared goals to unlock new monetization opportunities and maximize earnings potential.

**Invest in Quality Content**

Prioritize quality content creation and production to attract and retain listeners, enhance brand credibility, and command higher advertising rates and sponsorship deals. Focus on delivering valuable, engaging, and relevant content that resonates with your target audience and keeps them coming back for more.

**Focus on Audience Growth**

Invest in audience growth strategies to expand your reach, increase listener numbers, and attract potential advertisers and sponsors. Leverage social media, content marketing, SEO, and collaboration opportunities to reach new audiences and drive traffic to your podcast.

**Offer Premium Services**

Explore opportunities to offer premium services, consulting, coaching, or training based on your expertise, insights, and unique value proposition. Monetize your knowledge, skills, and experience through online courses, workshops, masterclasses, or personalized consulting services tailored to your audience's needs and interests.

**Explore Licensing and Syndication**

Explore licensing and syndication opportunities to monetize your podcast content beyond traditional advertising and sponsorships. License your content to third-party platforms, networks, or media outlets for distribution, syndication, or repackaging to reach new audiences and generate additional revenue streams.

## Monitor Industry Trends

Stay informed about industry trends, emerging technologies, and evolving consumer behaviors to anticipate market shifts, identify new monetization opportunities, and adapt your strategies accordingly. Stay agile, innovative, and proactive in responding to changes in the podcasting landscape to stay ahead of the competition and maximize earnings potential.

By implementing these strategies and tactics, podcasters can effectively measure, optimize, and maximize their revenue potential, turning their passion for podcasting into a sustainable and profitable venture.

# Chapter 9: Podcasting Best Practices

Podcasting success relies on implementing best practices that ensure quality, consistency, and engagement. In this chapter, we'll delve into various aspects of podcasting best practices to help you optimize your workflow, enhance listener experience, and achieve your goals.

# 9.1 Consistency and Scheduling

Consistency and scheduling are fundamental pillars of podcasting success. Establishing a regular release schedule and maintaining consistency in content delivery are essential for building audience trust, loyalty, and engagement. In this section, we'll explore strategies for maintaining consistency and effective scheduling in your podcasting endeavors.

## 9.1.1 Establishing a Regular Release Schedule

CONSISTENCY STARTS with establishing a regular release schedule for your podcast episodes. Whether you choose to release new episodes weekly, bi-weekly, or monthly, the key is to set a predictable cadence that aligns with your production capacity and audience preferences. Consider the following tips for establishing a regular release schedule:

**Understand Your Production Workflow**

Assess your production workflow, including recording, editing, and post-production processes, to determine a realistic release schedule. Factor in the time required for content creation, review, and publishing to ensure that you can consistently meet your chosen release cadence.

**Choose a Realistic Frequency**

Select a release frequency that you can sustain over the long term without compromising quality or burning out. While weekly releases are common, bi-weekly or monthly schedules may be more manageable depending on your resources, commitments, and content format.

**Communicate Your Schedule**

Clearly communicate your release schedule to your audience through your podcast website, social media channels, and episode descriptions. Set clear expectations regarding when new episodes will be available to help listeners anticipate and plan their listening habits accordingly.

**Stick to Your Schedule**

Once you've established a release schedule, strive to adhere to it consistently. Consistency builds trust and reliability with your audience, reinforcing their commitment to your podcast and increasing the likelihood of repeat listens and subscriptions.

## 9.1.2 Maintaining Consistency in Content Delivery

CONSISTENCY EXTENDS beyond release schedules to encompass the quality, format, and style of your podcast content. Maintaining consistency in content delivery involves delivering episodes that meet or exceed listener expectations while staying true to your podcast's brand and value proposition. Consider the following strategies for maintaining consistency in content delivery:

**Define Your Brand Identity**

Establish a clear brand identity for your podcast, including its tone, style, niche, and value proposition. Consistently align your content with your brand identity to create a cohesive listening experience and reinforce your podcast's unique identity and positioning in the market.

**Stick to Your Format**

Maintain consistency in your podcast format, structure, and episode length to provide listeners with a familiar and predictable experience. Whether you use a narrative format, interviews, discussions, or educational content, ensure that each episode adheres to your established format guidelines.

**Deliver on Expectations**

Understand your audience's expectations and preferences and strive to consistently deliver content that meets their needs and interests. Pay attention to listener feedback, engagement metrics, and market trends to refine your content strategy and ensure ongoing relevance and resonance with your audience.

## Quality Over Quantity

Prioritize quality over quantity when producing podcast episodes. While consistency is important, it's equally crucial to deliver high-quality content that engages, informs, and entertains your audience. Invest time and effort in crafting well-researched, well-produced episodes that provide value and leave a lasting impression on listeners.

## Monitor Performance and Feedback

Regularly monitor the performance of your podcast episodes, including listener engagement metrics, download numbers, and audience feedback. Use this data to evaluate the effectiveness of your content strategy, identify areas for improvement, and make data-driven decisions to optimize future episodes.

By prioritizing consistency and effective scheduling in your podcasting efforts, you can build a loyal audience, enhance listener engagement, and establish your podcast as a trusted source of valuable content within your niche.

# 9.2 Staying Informed and Adapting

In the dynamic landscape of podcasting, staying informed about industry trends, emerging technologies, and evolving audience preferences is essential for sustaining success and relevance. This section explores strategies for staying informed and adapting to changes in the podcasting ecosystem to optimize your podcasting endeavors.

## 9.2.1 Continuous Learning and Professional Development

PODCASTING IS AN EVER-evolving medium, with new technologies, strategies, and best practices constantly emerging. Engaging in continuous learning and professional development is crucial for podcasters to stay informed about the latest trends, tools, and techniques shaping the industry. Consider the following approaches to continuous learning:

**Podcasting Workshops and Courses**

Attend workshops, webinars, and online courses dedicated to podcasting topics such as content creation, production techniques, marketing strategies, and audience engagement. These educational opportunities provide valuable insights, practical skills, and networking opportunities with industry experts and fellow podcasters.

**Industry Conferences and Events**

Participate in podcasting conferences, summits, and industry events to stay abreast of the latest developments, trends, and innovations in the podcasting space. These gatherings offer opportunities to learn from industry leaders, discover new tools and technologies, and connect with peers to share insights and experiences.

**Podcasting Communities and Forums**

Join online communities, forums, and social media groups dedicated to podcasting to engage with fellow podcasters, exchange ideas, seek advice, and stay updated on industry news and discussions. Active participation in these communities fosters collaboration, networking, and knowledge-sharing within the podcasting community.

**Industry Publications and Resources**

Stay informed by regularly consuming industry publications, podcasts, blogs, and newsletters focused on podcasting. These resources provide valuable insights, analyses, case studies, and interviews with industry experts, helping you stay ahead of trends and developments shaping the podcasting landscape.

## 9.2.2 Monitoring Audience Feedback and Analytics

UNDERSTANDING YOUR audience is paramount to the success of your podcast. Regularly monitoring audience feedback, engagement metrics, and analytics provides valuable insights into listener preferences, behaviors, and demographics. Leveraging this data empowers you to adapt your content, strategies, and approaches to better serve your audience and achieve your podcasting goals. Consider the following practices for monitoring audience feedback and analytics:

**Listener Surveys and Feedback**

Conduct listener surveys, polls, and feedback sessions to gather insights into listener preferences, interests, and feedback regarding your podcast content, format, and delivery. Use this feedback to identify strengths, weaknesses, and areas for improvement, and tailor your content strategy accordingly.

**Analytics Platforms and Tools**

Utilize podcast analytics platforms and tools to track key performance indicators (KPIs) such as downloads, listens, audience demographics, listener retention, and engagement metrics. Analyze this data to assess the effectiveness of your content strategy, identify trends, and make data-driven decisions to optimize your podcasting efforts.

## Episode Performance Analysis

Evaluate the performance of individual episodes by analyzing download numbers, listener engagement, and audience feedback. Identify episodes that resonate particularly well with your audience and replicate successful elements in future content. Conversely, learn from episodes that underperform to avoid repeating mistakes and refine your approach.

## Social Media Listening

Monitor social media channels, podcast directories, and online communities for mentions, reviews, and discussions related to your podcast. Pay attention to audience sentiment, reactions, and conversations surrounding your content to gain valuable insights into audience perceptions, preferences, and trends.

## Competitor Analysis

Keep an eye on competitors and peers in your niche to understand their content strategies, audience engagement tactics, and marketing approaches. Identify emerging trends, successful strategies, and areas of opportunity to differentiate your podcast and stay competitive in the marketplace.

By staying informed about industry trends, monitoring audience feedback and analytics, and adapting your strategies based on insights and data, you can continually refine and optimize your podcasting efforts to better serve your audience and achieve your podcasting goals.

# 9.3 Maintaining Audio Quality

E nsuring high-quality audio is essential for creating a professional and engaging podcast experience. Poor audio quality can detract from your content, undermine listener satisfaction, and hinder the growth of your podcast. This section explores best practices for maintaining audio quality throughout the podcast production process.

## 9.3.1 Selecting Quality Equipment

INVESTING IN QUALITY recording equipment is the first step in achieving optimal audio quality for your podcast. Consider the following factors when selecting recording equipment:

**Microphones**

Choose microphones that are suitable for your recording environment and budget. Dynamic microphones are ideal for recording in non-sound-treated spaces, while condenser microphones offer higher sensitivity and detail capture in controlled environments. Select microphones known for their clarity, durability, and suitability for podcasting applications.

**Audio Interfaces and Mixers**

Use audio interfaces or mixers to connect microphones to your recording device or computer. Look for interfaces with clean preamps, low noise floors, and sufficient input/output options to accommodate your recording setup. Ensure compatibility with your microphones and recording software for seamless integration.

**Headphones**

Invest in quality headphones for monitoring audio during recording and editing. Closed-back headphones provide isolation from external noise, while open-back headphones offer a more natural soundstage. Choose headphones with accurate frequency response and comfortable wear for extended use.

**Recording Software**

Select recording software with features and capabilities that meet your podcasting needs. Look for software with multitrack recording, editing tools, real-time monitoring, and compatibility with your operating system and audio interface. Popular options include Audacity, Adobe Audition, GarageBand, and Reaper.

## 9.3.2 Optimizing Recording Environment

CREATING AN ACOUSTICALLY treated recording environment minimizes background noise, reflections, and other audio artifacts, resulting in cleaner recordings. Follow these tips to optimize your recording environment:

**Soundproofing**

Reduce external noise by soundproofing your recording space with acoustic panels, foam, blankets, or curtains. Focus on minimizing noise from HVAC systems, street traffic, and other sources of ambient noise.

**Acoustic Treatment**

Improve sound quality and reduce reflections by adding acoustic treatment to your recording space. Use bass traps, diffusers, and absorptive panels to minimize echoes, standing waves, and room modes that can color your recordings.

**Microphone Placement**

Position microphones correctly to capture clear and balanced audio. Experiment with microphone placement techniques such as the proximity effect, off-axis positioning, and distance from sound sources to achieve optimal sound capture.

**Monitoring**

Use headphones or studio monitors to monitor audio levels during recording. Maintain a comfortable listening volume to avoid clipping, distortion, and ear fatigue. Monitor audio in real-time to detect and address issues such as mic plosives, sibilance, and background noise.

### 9.3.3 Implementing Recording Best Practices

ADHERING TO BEST PRACTICES during recording ensures consistent audio quality and minimizes the need for extensive post-production editing. Follow these guidelines for optimal recording quality:

**Mic Technique**

Train podcast hosts and guests on proper microphone technique to maximize audio quality. Encourage consistent mic placement, proper posture, and uniform speaking distance to achieve consistent volume levels and tonal balance.

**Pacing and Delivery**

Coach podcast hosts and guests on pacing, articulation, and delivery to enhance clarity and engagement. Encourage natural speech patterns, avoid speaking too quickly or too softly, and emphasize enunciation to improve intelligibility.

**Monitoring Levels**

Monitor audio levels throughout the recording process to prevent clipping, distortion, and audio artifacts. Set appropriate gain levels on your audio interface or mixer to capture clean, distortion-free recordings without overloading the signal.

**Room Tone Capture**

Record several seconds of room tone at the beginning or end of each recording session to capture the ambient sound of your recording environment. Use room tone samples during post-production editing to fill gaps, smooth transitions, and maintain consistency in audio quality.

## Backup Recording

Always make backup recordings of your podcast sessions to mitigate the risk of data loss due to technical issues or equipment failure. Record redundant audio tracks using multiple recording devices or software applications to ensure continuity and reliability.

By selecting quality equipment, optimizing your recording environment, and implementing recording best practices, you can maintain high audio quality throughout the podcast production process, enhancing listener satisfaction and engagement.

# 9.4 Handling Feedback and Criticism

———

Feedback and criticism are inevitable aspects of creating and sharing content, including podcasts. While constructive feedback can help you improve your podcast and better serve your audience, handling criticism gracefully is essential for maintaining professionalism and fostering a positive podcasting experience. This section explores strategies for effectively managing feedback and criticism in the podcasting realm.

## 9.4.1 Embracing Constructive Feedback

CONSTRUCTIVE FEEDBACK provides valuable insights into your podcast's strengths and areas for improvement. Embrace constructive criticism as an opportunity for growth and refinement. Consider the following tips for handling constructive feedback:

☑ **Listen with an Open Mind**: Approach feedback with a willingness to listen and learn. Keep an open mind and resist the urge to dismiss or downplay criticism. Acknowledge valid points raised by listeners and consider how you can address them to enhance your podcast.

☑ **Seek Clarification**: If feedback is unclear or ambiguous, don't hesitate to seek clarification from the individual providing it. Ask specific questions to better understand their perspective and gather actionable insights for improvement.

☑ **Identify Patterns**: Look for recurring themes or patterns in feedback received from multiple listeners. Common themes may indicate areas where your podcast excels or areas needing attention. Use patterns to prioritize feedback and focus on changes that will have the greatest impact.

☑ **Express Gratitude:** Show appreciation to listeners who take the time to provide feedback, regardless of its nature. Thank them for their input and acknowledge their role in helping you refine your podcast. Expressing gratitude fosters goodwill and encourages continued engagement.

## 9.4.2 Responding to Criticism Professionally

CRITICISM, WHETHER constructive or negative, can be challenging to receive, especially when it feels personal or unjustified. Responding to criticism professionally is essential for preserving your podcast's reputation and maintaining positive relationships with your audience. Consider the following strategies for responding to criticism effectively:

### Remain Calm and Objective

When faced with criticism, take a step back and assess the feedback objectively. Avoid reacting impulsively or defensively, as this may escalate tensions and exacerbate the situation. Maintain a calm and composed demeanor in your response.

### Acknowledge Validity

Even if you disagree with the criticism, acknowledge its validity and the perspective of the individual providing it. Validating their concerns demonstrates empathy and respect, even if you ultimately choose not to act on their feedback.

### Provide Context or Explanation

If criticism is based on misunderstandings or misinterpretations, provide context or explanation to clarify your intentions or actions. Clear communication can help address misconceptions and alleviate concerns raised by listeners.

### Apologize When Necessary

If your podcast or actions have genuinely caused harm or offense, offer a sincere apology to affected individuals. Acknowledge any mistakes or missteps on your part and express a commitment to rectifying the situation and preventing similar issues in the future.

### Focus on Solutions

Shift the focus of the conversation from criticism to solutions. Instead of dwelling on past mistakes or shortcomings, discuss actionable steps for improvement and how you plan to address feedback moving forward. Demonstrating a proactive approach can help rebuild trust and confidence among your audience.

## 9.4.3 Cultivating Resilience and Self-Confidence

HANDLING FEEDBACK AND criticism in the podcasting realm requires resilience and self-confidence. Embrace challenges as opportunities for growth and view criticism as a natural part of the creative process. Cultivate resilience by:

### Building a Support Network

Surround yourself with mentors, peers, and fellow podcasters who can offer support, guidance, and encouragement. Lean on your support network during challenging times and seek their perspective on handling feedback and criticism.

### Practicing Self-Compassion

Be kind to yourself and practice self-compassion when faced with criticism. Recognize that perfection is unattainable, and mistakes are an inevitable part of the learning process. Treat yourself with the same kindness and understanding you would offer to others.

### Celebrating Achievements

Celebrate your podcasting achievements and milestones, no matter how small. Recognize your progress and growth as a podcaster and acknowledge the impact your podcast has had on your audience. Celebrating achievements boosts morale and reinforces your dedication to podcasting.

## Maintaining Perspective

Keep feedback and criticism in perspective by focusing on the bigger picture. Remember why you started podcasting and the goals you hope to achieve with your content. Maintain a long-term outlook and avoid getting bogged down by short-term setbacks or challenges.

Handling feedback and criticism effectively is an essential skill for podcasters seeking to grow and improve their craft. By embracing constructive feedback, responding to criticism professionally, and cultivating resilience and self-confidence, you can navigate the ups and downs of podcasting with grace and determination.

# 9.5 Staying Committed for the Long Haul

———

Maintaining a successful podcast requires dedication, perseverance, and a long-term commitment to your craft. In this section, we'll explore strategies for staying motivated and committed to podcasting over the long haul.

## 9.5.1 Clarifying Your Why

BEFORE EMBARKING ON your podcasting journey, it's essential to clarify your why—the underlying purpose or motivation driving your podcast. Understanding why you're podcasting can help you stay committed when faced with challenges or setbacks. Consider the following steps for clarifying your why:

❖ **Reflect on Your Motivations:** Take time to reflect on why you're passionate about podcasting and what you hope to achieve with your content. Identify the values, interests, or goals that drive your podcasting efforts.

❖ **Define Your Objectives:** Clearly define your podcasting objectives, whether they involve educating, entertaining, inspiring, or informing your audience. Establishing clear goals can provide direction and focus as you navigate the complexities of podcasting.

❖ **Connect with Your Audience:** Consider the impact you hope to have on your audience and how your podcast can enrich their lives. Building meaningful connections with your listeners can reinforce your commitment to podcasting and provide a sense of purpose.

## 9.5.2 Cultivating Consistency

CONSISTENCY IS KEY to building a loyal audience and maintaining momentum in podcasting. Whether it's releasing episodes on a regular schedule or adhering to a consistent format, cultivating consistency can help you establish trust and reliability with your listeners. Here are some tips for staying consistent:

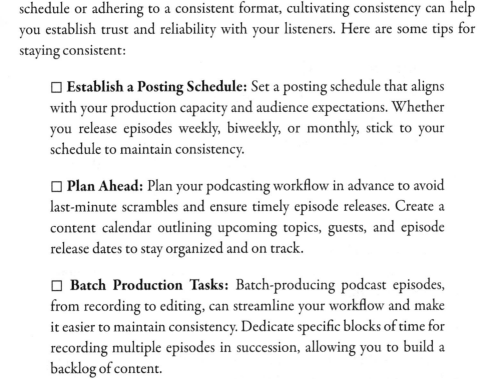

☐ **Establish a Posting Schedule:** Set a posting schedule that aligns with your production capacity and audience expectations. Whether you release episodes weekly, biweekly, or monthly, stick to your schedule to maintain consistency.

☐ **Plan Ahead:** Plan your podcasting workflow in advance to avoid last-minute scrambles and ensure timely episode releases. Create a content calendar outlining upcoming topics, guests, and episode release dates to stay organized and on track.

☐ **Batch Production Tasks:** Batch-producing podcast episodes, from recording to editing, can streamline your workflow and make it easier to maintain consistency. Dedicate specific blocks of time for recording multiple episodes in succession, allowing you to build a backlog of content.

## 9.5.3 Embracing Flexibility

WHILE CONSISTENCY IS important, it's also essential to embrace flexibility and adaptability in podcasting. Unexpected challenges, changes in audience preferences, or personal circumstances may require adjustments to your podcasting approach. Here's how to embrace flexibility:

**Stay Agile**

Remain flexible and open to change as you navigate the evolving landscape of podcasting. Be willing to experiment with new formats, topics, or styles based on audience feedback and emerging trends.

**Anticipate Challenges**

Recognize that challenges are inevitable in podcasting and develop strategies for overcoming them. Whether it's technical difficulties, scheduling conflicts, or creative blocks, anticipate potential challenges and devise contingency plans to address them.

## 9.5.4 Cultivating Self-Care

PODCASTING CAN BE DEMANDING, both physically and mentally, so prioritizing self-care is crucial for maintaining long-term commitment and well-being. Incorporate self-care practices into your podcasting routine to avoid burnout and sustain your passion for podcasting. Consider the following self-care strategies:

### Set Boundaries

Establish clear boundaries around your podcasting commitments to prevent overwhelm and burnout. Schedule regular breaks, set limits on work hours, and prioritize activities that recharge your energy and creativity.

### Practice Mindfulness

Incorporate mindfulness practices, such as meditation, deep breathing, or mindful movement, into your daily routine to reduce stress and increase resilience. Cultivating mindfulness can help you stay present, focused, and grounded amidst the demands of podcasting.

### Seek Support

Don't hesitate to reach out for support from friends, family, or fellow podcasters when needed. Surround yourself with a supportive network who can offer encouragement, advice, and perspective during challenging times.

By clarifying your why, cultivating consistency, embracing flexibility, and prioritizing self-care, you can stay committed to podcasting for the long haul. Remember that success in podcasting is not just about achieving specific milestones but also about enjoying the journey and making meaningful connections with your audience along the way.

# Chapter 10: Navigating Challenges and Pitfalls

# 10.1 Technical Challenges and Solutions

Navigating the technical landscape of podcasting can be a daunting task, but being prepared to address common challenges ensures smoother production processes. Here are some key technical challenges podcasters may encounter, along with solutions to mitigate their impact:

**Addressing Audio Quality Issues**

Achieving high-quality audio is paramount in podcasting. Invest in quality microphones, use acoustic treatments to minimize room noise, and employ audio editing techniques to enhance clarity and remove background noise.

**Dealing with Recording and Editing Software Problems**

Software glitches or crashes can disrupt recording and editing sessions. Ensure that all software components are up to date, regularly save your work, and consider using reliable backup software or cloud storage solutions to prevent data loss.

**Troubleshooting Common Podcasting Equipment Issues**

From microphones to mixers, podcasting equipment can encounter various issues such as connectivity problems or hardware malfunctions. Familiarize yourself with troubleshooting procedures provided by equipment manufacturers and have backup equipment on hand to minimize downtime.

**Ensuring a Stable Internet Connection**

Reliable internet connectivity is essential, especially for remote interviews or live streaming. Use wired connections whenever possible, invest in quality routers and modems, and have a backup internet connection available as a contingency plan.

**Backing Up and Securing Podcast Files**

Protecting your podcast files from loss or corruption is crucial. Implement a robust backup strategy, including regular backups to external drives or cloud storage platforms. Consider encryption and password protection to safeguard sensitive podcasting assets.

## Additional Considerations

### Software Compatibility

Ensure compatibility between recording, editing, and publishing platforms, and regularly test software updates to pre-emptively identify and address compatibility issues.

### Testing Procedures

Develop a comprehensive testing protocol to identify potential technical issues before recording sessions or live broadcasts, and regularly test equipment, software, and internet connections to maintain optimal performance.

### Remote Recording Considerations

Provide clear instructions and technical support for remote interviews or collaborations and communicate with guests or co-hosts in advance to troubleshoot setup and compatibility issues.

### Technical Support Resources

Utilize online forums, user communities, and technical support resources provided by equipment manufacturers and software developers for troubleshooting tips and solutions.

### Continuous Learning

Stay updated on emerging technologies and best practices in podcast production through online courses, webinars, and industry publications to optimize your podcasting workflow and address evolving technical challenges effectively.

### Documenting Solutions

Keep detailed records of encountered technical issues and implemented solutions for future reference, streamlining problem-solving processes and maintaining podcasting integrity.

By proactively addressing technical challenges and leveraging these additional considerations, podcasters can navigate the intricacies of podcast production with confidence and ensure the consistent delivery of high-quality content to their audiences.

# 10.2 Content Creation Challenges

———

Creating compelling content is a core aspect of podcasting success, but it comes with its own set of challenges. From writer's block to content fatigue, podcasters often face hurdles in generating fresh and engaging topics consistently. Here are some common content creation challenges and strategies for overcoming them:

**Overcoming Writer's Block or Content Fatigue**

Writer's block can stall creativity and hinder content production. Experiment with different brainstorming techniques, take breaks to recharge, and explore alternative creative outlets to stimulate inspiration. Collaborating with co-hosts or inviting guest speakers can inject fresh perspectives and ideas into your content.

**Finding Fresh and Engaging Topics**

Sourcing new and captivating topics can be challenging, especially for long-running podcasts. Stay curious and receptive to inspiration from various sources such as current events, audience feedback, industry trends, and personal experiences. Conduct audience surveys or polls to gather insights into topics that resonate with your listeners.

**Balancing Consistency with Content Quality**

Maintaining consistency in content delivery while upholding quality standards requires careful planning and organization. Develop a content calendar or schedule to outline episode topics and publication dates, allowing for flexibility to accommodate unforeseen circumstances. Prioritize content quality over quantity and allocate sufficient time for research, scripting, and production.

**Managing Time and Workload Effectively**

Podcasting often entails juggling multiple roles and responsibilities, leading to time management challenges. Implement time-blocking techniques, set realistic deadlines, and delegate tasks where possible to streamline workflows and minimize overwhelm. Utilize productivity tools and project management systems to track progress and prioritize tasks efficiently.

### Handling Content Burnout and Rejuvenation Strategies

Sustaining creativity and motivation over the long term can be challenging, leading to content burnout. Practice self-care techniques such as mindfulness, exercise, and adequate rest to prevent burnout and maintain mental well-being. Incorporate variety into your content format, experiment with new formats or segments, and take occasional breaks to recharge and reignite enthusiasm.

## Additional Considerations

### Audience Engagement and Feedback

Stay attuned to audience preferences and feedback to tailor content to their interests and needs. Encourage listener interaction through surveys, Q&A sessions, and community forums to foster a sense of ownership and involvement.

### Research and Preparation

Invest time in thorough research and preparation to ensure the accuracy and relevance of your content. Engage with industry experts, conduct interviews, and cite credible sources to provide valuable insights and perspectives to your audience.

### Continuous Learning and Growth

Commit to ongoing learning and skill development in content creation techniques, storytelling, and audience engagement strategies. Attend workshops, enroll in online courses, and seek mentorship opportunities to refine your craft and adapt to evolving trends and technologies.

### Experimentation and Innovation

Embrace experimentation and innovation in content creation to differentiate your podcast and keep it fresh and dynamic. Explore multimedia formats, storytelling techniques, and emerging technologies to captivate your audience and stay ahead of the curve.

By acknowledging and addressing these content creation challenges, podcasters can enhance the quality and relevance of their content, strengthen audience engagement, and sustain long-term success in the competitive podcasting landscape.

# 10.3 Audience Engagement and Growth Hurdles

Building and sustaining an engaged audience is vital for the success of any podcast, but it comes with its own set of challenges. From attracting new listeners to fostering community engagement and managing feedback, podcasters encounter various hurdles along the journey. Here are some common audience engagement and growth challenges and strategies for overcoming them:

## Strategies for Growing and Retaining Your Audience

Growing your audience requires a multifaceted approach that combines content quality, promotion, and audience interaction. Utilize social media platforms, email newsletters, and cross-promotion with other podcasts to expand your reach. Offer valuable incentives such as exclusive content, giveaways, or guest appearances to incentivize audience loyalty and retention.

## Dealing with Negative Feedback and Criticism

Negative feedback and criticism are inevitable in the public sphere of podcasting. Approach criticism constructively by seeking opportunities for improvement and learning from feedback. Develop resilience and emotional intelligence to handle criticism gracefully, focusing on constructive dialogue and growth rather than personal attacks.

## Challenges in Fostering Community Engagement

Building a vibrant community around your podcast requires ongoing effort and engagement. Encourage listener participation through interactive segments, listener Q&A sessions, and community forums. Foster a sense of belonging and inclusivity by acknowledging and valuing listener contributions, feedback, and opinions.

## Navigating Through Fluctuations in Listener Numbers

Fluctuations in listener numbers are a common challenge for podcasters, influenced by factors such as content relevance, promotion efforts, and external events. Stay proactive in monitoring audience metrics and identifying trends to understand fluctuations and adapt strategies accordingly. Focus on long-term audience growth rather than short-term fluctuations, maintaining consistency in content quality and engagement.

### Addressing Podcast Marketing and Promotion Obstacles

Marketing and promoting your podcast effectively can be challenging, especially with limited resources and competition in the podcasting landscape. Experiment with different marketing channels such as social media advertising, influencer partnerships, and SEO optimization to increase visibility and reach. Collaborate with niche communities, industry influencers, and relevant media outlets to amplify your podcast's reach and attract new listeners.

## Additional Considerations

### Building Brand Authority and Trust

Establishing credibility and trustworthiness is essential for attracting and retaining listeners. Consistently deliver valuable, high-quality content that aligns with your brand values and resonates with your target audience. Engage in thought leadership activities such as speaking engagements, guest appearances on other podcasts, and publishing authoritative content to reinforce your brand authority and expertise.

### Diversifying Content Formats and Platforms

Explore diverse content formats and distribution channels to reach and engage with different audience segments. Experiment with multimedia content such as video podcasts, live streams, and interactive experiences to cater to diverse preferences and consumption habits. Leverage emerging platforms and technologies to stay ahead of the curve and expand your podcast's reach beyond traditional audio formats.

### Community Building and Engagement Strategies

Cultivate a sense of community among your listeners by fostering meaningful connections and interactions. Encourage user-generated content, host virtual meetups or events, and facilitate peer-to-peer networking opportunities to deepen engagement and loyalty. Actively listen to audience feedback and incorporate their suggestions and preferences into your content and community initiatives.

## Data-Driven Decision Making

Utilize analytics and audience insights to inform strategic decision-making and optimize engagement strategies. Track key performance indicators (KPIs) such as listener demographics, engagement metrics, and conversion rates to gauge the effectiveness of your audience engagement efforts. Iterate and refine your strategies based on data-driven insights to continuously improve audience engagement and growth outcomes.

By proactively addressing these audience engagement and growth hurdles, podcasters can cultivate a loyal and engaged audience, drive sustainable growth, and maximize the impact of their podcast in the competitive podcasting landscape.

# 10.4 Monetization and Revenue Challenges

———

**M**onetizing a podcast is a goal for many creators, but it comes with its own set of challenges and considerations. From exploring various monetization options to managing financial aspects and navigating sponsorship hurdles, podcasters encounter several challenges along the path to generating revenue. Here are some common monetization and revenue challenges and strategies for addressing them:

## Options and Challenges in Monetizing Your Podcast

Podcasters have various options for monetizing their content, including advertising, sponsorships, premium subscriptions, merchandise sales, donations, and crowdfunding. However, each monetization method presents its own challenges, such as finding suitable advertisers, attracting paying subscribers, or managing inventory for merchandise sales. Evaluate the pros and cons of each monetization option and choose strategies that align with your audience, content, and goals.

## Dealing with Sponsorship and Advertising Hurdles

Securing sponsorships and advertising deals can be challenging, especially for smaller podcasts or niche content. Overcoming hurdles such as low listener numbers, lack of brand awareness, or competition from established podcasts requires proactive outreach, compelling pitch proposals, and demonstrating the value proposition of your podcast to potential sponsors. Consider alternative sponsorship models such as affiliate marketing, native advertising, or direct sponsorships to diversify revenue streams and increase monetization opportunities.

## Strategies for Setting and Justifying Pricing for Premium Content

Offering premium content or subscription-based services can be an effective monetization strategy but determining pricing and justifying the value proposition to your audience are key challenges. Conduct market research to understand pricing benchmarks and audience willingness to pay for premium content. Clearly communicate the benefits and exclusive features of premium offerings, such as ad-free episodes, bonus content, early access, or exclusive merchandise, to justify pricing and incentivize subscriptions.

### Challenges in Diversifying Revenue Streams

Relying on a single monetization method can be risky, as it leaves podcasters vulnerable to fluctuations in market conditions or changes in audience preferences. Diversifying revenue streams by exploring multiple monetization options, such as sponsorships, subscriptions, merchandise sales, and crowdfunding, can help mitigate risk and maximize revenue potential. However, managing multiple revenue streams requires careful planning, resource allocation, and balancing the needs and expectations of different stakeholders.

### Handling Financial Aspects, Taxes, and Expenses

Managing the financial aspects of podcasting, including revenue tracking, budgeting, taxation, and expense management, can be complex and time-consuming. Implementing accounting systems, hiring financial professionals, and staying informed about tax regulations and compliance requirements are essential for ensuring financial stability and sustainability. Keep detailed records of income and expenses, explore tax deductions for podcasting-related expenses, and allocate resources strategically to maximize profitability and minimize financial risk.

## Additional Considerations

### Navigating Legal and Regulatory Compliance

Monetizing your podcast involves navigating legal and regulatory requirements related to advertising disclosures, privacy policies, copyright and intellectual property rights, and compliance with industry standards and guidelines. Stay informed about relevant laws and regulations governing podcast monetization and seek legal advice or guidance when necessary to ensure compliance and mitigate legal risks.

## Building Trust and Credibility with Your Audience

Maintaining trust and credibility with your audience is essential for successful monetization efforts. Be transparent about your monetization methods, disclose sponsored content or affiliate relationships clearly, and prioritize the interests and needs of your audience. Deliver high-quality content consistently, engage authentically with your audience, and prioritize listener satisfaction to build a loyal and supportive community that is receptive to your monetization initiatives.

## Continuous Evaluation and Optimization

Monitor and evaluate the performance of your monetization strategies regularly, analyzing key metrics such as revenue growth, conversion rates, subscriber retention, and audience feedback. Identify areas for improvement and optimization, experiment with new monetization tactics or revenue streams, and adapt your strategies based on evolving market trends, audience preferences, and competitive dynamics. Stay agile and proactive in adjusting your monetization approach to maximize revenue generation and long-term sustainability.

By addressing these monetization and revenue challenges strategically and proactively, podcasters can navigate the complexities of monetizing their content effectively, unlock new revenue opportunities, and build a sustainable business model that supports their podcasting endeavors for the long term.

# 10.5 Legal and Copyright Issues

———

Podcasting, like any form of content creation, comes with legal responsibilities and considerations. Understanding copyright laws, intellectual property rights, and privacy regulations is crucial for podcasters to avoid legal pitfalls and protect their content. Here are some key legal and copyright issues podcasters may encounter and strategies for addressing them:

## Understanding Copyright and Intellectual Property Rights

Podcasters must understand copyright laws and intellectual property rights to ensure they have the legal right to use and distribute their content. Familiarize yourself with copyright basics, including what constitutes copyrighted material, fair use principles, and licensing requirements for using third-party content. Respect the intellectual property rights of others and obtain proper permissions or licenses when using copyrighted material in your podcast.

## Avoiding Legal Pitfalls Related to Music and Media Usage

Music and media usage in podcasts require careful consideration to avoid copyright infringement. Use royalty-free music, creative commons-licensed content, or tracks from reputable music libraries to avoid legal issues related to music usage. Be cautious when using copyrighted material such as movie clips, sound effects, or audio snippets, and seek permission or licenses from rights holders when necessary. Consider working with musicians, composers, or production companies to create original music or sound effects for your podcast to ensure compliance with copyright laws.

## Dealing with Copyright Infringement Claims

Infringement claims can arise if podcasters use copyrighted material without proper authorization, potentially leading to legal consequences such as takedown notices, cease-and-desist letters, or lawsuits. Take prompt action to address infringement claims by removing infringing content, responding to legal notices, and seeking legal advice if necessary. Be proactive in understanding your rights and responsibilities as a content creator and prioritize compliance with copyright laws to avoid legal disputes.

## Complying with Privacy and Data Protection Regulations

Podcasters must adhere to privacy and data protection regulations when collecting, storing, or processing personal information from listeners or guests. Implement privacy policies and data protection measures to safeguard sensitive information and ensure compliance with applicable laws such as the General Data Protection Regulation (GDPR) or the California Consumer Privacy Act (CCPA). Obtain consent from individuals before collecting their personal data and handle sensitive information responsibly to maintain trust and transparency with your audience.

## Navigating Through Podcasting Contracts and Agreements

Podcasters may encounter various contracts and agreements in their podcasting journey, including licensing agreements, sponsorship contracts, guest release forms, or distribution agreements. Review contracts carefully, seek legal advice if needed, and negotiate terms that protect your rights and interests. Clarify ownership rights, usage permissions, payment terms, and dispute resolution mechanisms to avoid misunderstandings or conflicts down the line. Maintain clear communication and documentation throughout the contracting process to ensure mutual understanding and compliance with contractual obligations.

# Additional Considerations

## Staying Informed About Legal Developments

Keep abreast of legal developments, industry standards, and best practices related to podcasting and content creation. Stay informed about changes to copyright laws, privacy regulations, or industry guidelines that may affect your podcasting activities. Attend legal seminars, participate in industry forums, and seek guidance from legal experts or professional organizations to stay updated on emerging legal issues and compliance requirements relevant to podcasting.

## Seeking Legal Advice When Needed

When in doubt or facing complex legal issues, don't hesitate to seek legal advice from qualified attorneys specializing in intellectual property, media law, or entertainment law. Legal experts can provide personalized guidance, assess legal risks, and offer practical solutions tailored to your specific circumstances. Invest in legal counsel to protect your rights, mitigate legal liabilities, and navigate through legal challenges effectively, ensuring the long-term success and sustainability of your podcasting endeavors.

By understanding and proactively addressing legal and copyright issues, podcasters can protect their content, mitigate legal risks, and build a solid legal foundation for their podcasting activities. Compliance with copyright laws, intellectual property rights, and privacy regulations is essential for maintaining trust with your audience, preserving the integrity of your content, and avoiding costly legal disputes that could jeopardize your podcasting endeavors.

# Chapter 11: The Future of Podcasting

As the podcasting landscape continues to evolve, it's essential for podcasters to stay informed about emerging trends and technologies shaping the industry's future. In this chapter, we'll explore the latest developments and innovations driving podcasting forward, empowering creators to adapt and thrive in an ever-changing digital landscape.

# 11.1 Emerging Trends and Technologies

———

$\mathrm{T}$he podcasting industry is witnessing rapid advancements and transformative changes fueled by technological innovation, shifting consumer behaviors, and evolving content consumption habits. Here are some emerging trends and technologies reshaping the future of podcasting:

### Interactive Podcasting Experiences

With the rise of interactive content and immersive storytelling, podcasters are exploring new ways to engage listeners through interactive experiences. Emerging technologies such as voice-controlled devices, augmented reality (AR), and virtual reality (VR) are enabling podcasters to create interactive narratives, gamified content, and participatory experiences that blur the lines between storytelling and audience engagement. Experiment with interactive storytelling formats, interactive audio dramas, or choose-your-own-adventure podcasts to captivate audiences and enhance listener engagement.

### Personalized Content Recommendations

As podcast libraries expand and listener preferences diversify, personalized content recommendations and discovery algorithms are becoming increasingly important for helping listeners find relevant and engaging podcasts. Leveraging machine learning algorithms, data analytics, and listener behavior insights, podcast platforms are enhancing their recommendation engines to deliver personalized content suggestions tailored to individual tastes, interests, and listening habits. Incorporate metadata optimization, user engagement data analysis, and personalized recommendation algorithms to optimize discoverability and attract new listeners to your podcast.

### Enhanced Audio Production Techniques

With advancements in audio production technologies and techniques, podcasters have access to a wide range of tools and resources for creating high-quality audio content. From immersive 3D audio experiences and binaural recording techniques to spatial audio processing and dynamic soundscapes, podcasters can leverage cutting-edge audio production techniques to enhance storytelling, create immersive atmospheres, and captivate audiences with rich, multi-dimensional audio experiences. Experiment with spatial audio formats, ambisonic sound design, or interactive audio elements to push the boundaries of audio storytelling and deliver captivating content to your listeners.

## Monetization Innovations

As podcasting matures as a medium, new monetization models and revenue streams are emerging to support creators and sustainably monetize their content. In addition to traditional advertising and sponsorship models, podcasters are exploring innovative monetization strategies such as premium subscriptions, exclusive content offerings, merchandise sales, live events, and direct listener support platforms. Embrace diversification in your monetization approach, experiment with hybrid revenue models, and explore niche opportunities to maximize revenue potential and create sustainable income streams from your podcasting efforts.

## AI-Powered Content Creation and Automation

Artificial intelligence (AI) and machine learning technologies are revolutionizing content creation, automation, and production workflows in the podcasting industry. AI-powered tools and platforms are enabling podcasters to automate repetitive tasks, streamline production processes, and enhance content quality through automated transcription, editing, voice synthesis, and content analysis capabilities. Incorporate AI-driven solutions into your podcasting workflow to increase efficiency, scale production efforts, and unlock new creative possibilities while minimizing manual labor and resource requirements.

## Cross-Platform Distribution and Syndication

With the proliferation of podcast platforms and distribution channels, podcasters are embracing cross-platform distribution and syndication strategies to reach wider audiences and maximize their content's reach. Leveraging podcast hosting platforms, content syndication networks, and distribution aggregators, podcasters can distribute their content across multiple platforms, directories, and channels simultaneously, ensuring broad visibility, discoverability, and accessibility for their podcasts. Optimize your podcast distribution strategy, syndicate your content across diverse platforms, and explore partnerships with distribution networks to expand your podcast's reach and audience engagement.

## Emergence of Niche and Specialized Content

As the podcasting landscape becomes increasingly saturated with content, niche and specialized podcasts catering to specific interests, demographics, and communities are gaining prominence. Podcasters are tapping into niche markets, underserved audiences, and specialized content genres to differentiate their podcasts, build loyal audiences, and foster niche communities around their content. Identify unique niches, untapped audience segments, or specialized topics aligned with your expertise and passions to carve out a distinct niche in the podcasting ecosystem and establish yourself as a thought leader or authority in your niche domain.

## Live and Interactive Podcasting Platforms

Live and interactive podcasting platforms are gaining traction, allowing podcasters to engage with their audience in real-time, foster community interaction, and create dynamic, interactive content experiences. Live streaming platforms, interactive audio chat apps, and virtual event platforms offer podcasters new opportunities to connect with listeners, host live Q&A sessions, conduct interactive discussions, and collaborate with guests or co-hosts in real-time. Experiment with live podcasting formats, interactive audience participation features, and virtual event hosting to engage your audience, cultivate community engagement, and create memorable live experiences that resonate with your listeners.

## Blockchain and Decentralized Content Distribution

Blockchain technology and decentralized content distribution platforms are disrupting traditional media distribution models, offering podcasters decentralized, censorship-resistant alternatives for publishing, distributing, and monetizing their content. Blockchain-based podcasting platforms leverage blockchain technology to enable transparent, peer-to-peer content distribution, immutable content ownership, and decentralized micropayments, empowering creators to retain greater control over their content, monetization, and audience relationships. Explore blockchain-based podcasting platforms, decentralized content networks, and cryptocurrency-based monetization models to embrace the principles of decentralization, transparency, and sovereignty in your podcasting endeavors.

## Ethical Considerations and Responsible Content Creation

As podcasting continues to grow in influence and reach, podcasters must prioritize ethical considerations, responsible content creation practices, and social responsibility in their podcasting efforts. Uphold journalistic integrity, ethical storytelling principles, and responsible content creation practices to build trust, credibility, and authenticity with your audience. Consider the ethical implications of your content, respect diverse perspectives, and foster inclusivity, diversity, and representation in your podcasting content to create a positive impact, promote social change, and contribute to a more inclusive and equitable podcasting ecosystem.

By staying informed about emerging trends and technologies, embracing innovation, and adopting forward-thinking strategies, podcasters can position themselves for success in an evolving podcasting landscape, unlock new opportunities for growth and innovation, and shape the future of podcasting as a dynamic and thriving medium for creative expression, storytelling, and community engagement.

# 11.2 Diversification of Podcast Content

―――

As the podcasting landscape evolves, content diversification plays a pivotal role in shaping the future trajectory of the medium. In this chapter, we delve into the significance of diversifying podcast content and explore various strategies and trends driving this evolution.

Podcasting has evolved far beyond its origins of long-form interviews and storytelling. Content diversification is essential for catering to diverse audience interests, expanding reach, and staying relevant in an increasingly competitive landscape. Here are key aspects of content diversification in podcasting:

### Genre Expansion and Specialized Niches

While true crime, comedy, and interview-style podcasts continue to dominate the medium, there's a growing trend towards genre expansion and niche specialization. Podcasters are exploring diverse genres such as history, science fiction, personal development, true stories, business, wellness, and niche topics catering to specific hobbies, interests, and communities. By tapping into specialized niches, podcasters can carve out a distinct identity, attract loyal audiences, and differentiate their content in a crowded market.

### Serialized Storytelling and Serialized Formats

Serialized storytelling has gained popularity, with podcasters adopting episodic formats akin to television series or serialized novels. Serialized podcasts offer immersive narrative experiences, unfolding complex story arcs, character development, and plot twists over multiple episodes. From fictional dramas and mystery thrillers to investigative journalism and documentary series, serialized storytelling captivates listeners with compelling narratives, cliffhangers, and suspense, encouraging binge-listening and audience engagement.

### Short-Form and Micro-Podcasting

In contrast to traditional long-form podcasts, short-form and micro-podcasting formats are gaining traction, catering to audiences seeking bite-sized content for on-the-go consumption. Short form podcasts typically feature concise episodes ranging from a few minutes to under 20 minutes, delivering quick insights, tips, news updates, or entertaining anecdotes. Micro-podcasts, often less than five minutes in length, offer ultra-short bursts of content, perfect for brief commutes, coffee breaks, or daily inspiration. Embracing short-form and micro-podcasting formats allows podcasters to accommodate shorter attention spans, reach new audiences, and experiment with diverse content formats.

## Multimedia and Cross-Platform Integration

Podcasting is expanding beyond audio-only formats, embracing multimedia content and cross-platform integration to enhance storytelling and audience engagement. Video podcasts, live streams, interactive content, companion websites, blogs, newsletters, and social media integration complement audio content, providing listeners with additional context, visual aids, supplementary materials, and interactive experiences. By leveraging multimedia formats and cross-platform integration, podcasters can enrich their content, extend their reach, and foster deeper connections with their audience across multiple channels and platforms.

## Branded and Sponsored Content

As podcasting matures as a medium, branded and sponsored content collaborations are becoming increasingly prevalent, offering podcasters new monetization opportunities and diversifying content offerings. Branded podcasts, sponsored series, and branded content integrations enable podcasters to collaborate with brands, organizations, and sponsors to create custom content aligned with brand values, target audience interests, and campaign objectives. By incorporating branded and sponsored content into their podcasting strategy, creators can generate revenue, support production costs, and deliver valuable, branded storytelling experiences to their audience.

## Interactive and Participatory Experiences

Podcasting platforms and technologies are enabling interactive and participatory experiences, allowing listeners to engage with content, influence narratives, and participate in storytelling in unprecedented ways. Live podcasts, interactive polls, audience Q&A sessions, listener call-ins, virtual events, and community-driven initiatives empower listeners to become active participants in the content creation process, fostering community engagement, building relationships, and cultivating a sense of belonging within podcasting communities. By embracing interactive and participatory experiences, podcasters can deepen audience engagement, drive listener loyalty, and create immersive content experiences that resonate with their audience.

## Cultural and Linguistic Diversity

As podcasting continues to globalize, there's a growing emphasis on cultural and linguistic diversity, with podcasters creating content in multiple languages, dialects, and cultural contexts. Podcasts produced by underrepresented voices, marginalized communities, and diverse creators offer unique perspectives, authentic storytelling, and rich cultural insights, enriching the podcasting landscape with diverse voices and narratives. By promoting cultural and linguistic diversity, podcasters can foster inclusivity, broaden audience reach, and contribute to a more diverse and equitable podcasting ecosystem.

Diversifying podcast content is essential for driving innovation, expanding audience reach, and staying competitive in an ever-evolving podcasting landscape. By embracing diverse content formats, genres, platforms, and perspectives, podcasters can captivate audiences, foster community engagement, and shape the future of podcasting as a dynamic and inclusive medium for storytelling, education, and entertainment.

# 11.3 Expanding International Reach

In the rapidly evolving landscape of podcasting, expanding international reach is paramount for creators looking to broaden their audience base, foster global connections, and capitalize on emerging markets. This section explores strategies, trends, and considerations for expanding international reach in podcasting.

With the global reach of the internet and the ubiquity of smartphones, podcasting has become a truly international medium, transcending geographical boundaries and language barriers. Expanding international reach offers podcasters opportunities for growth, cultural exchange, and cross-cultural dialogue. Here are key aspects to consider when expanding international reach in podcasting:

## Localization and Multilingual Content

One of the most effective strategies for reaching international audiences is localization and offering multilingual content. Podcasters can translate their episodes, titles, and descriptions into multiple languages to cater to diverse language preferences and cultural contexts. Providing localized content allows podcasters to connect with audiences worldwide, increase discoverability in international markets, and overcome language barriers. Moreover, producing episodes in different languages enables podcasters to engage with multicultural audiences, foster inclusivity, and amplify diverse voices and perspectives.

## Cultural Sensitivity and Adaptation

Understanding cultural nuances, norms, and sensitivities is essential when expanding international reach. Podcasters should adapt their content, messaging, and marketing strategies to resonate with diverse cultural backgrounds and preferences. Conducting thorough research on target markets, cultural customs, and audience preferences can help podcasters tailor their content effectively, avoid cultural missteps, and build authentic connections with international audiences. Embracing cultural diversity and inclusivity fosters goodwill, enhances audience engagement, and strengthens global brand presence in the podcasting community.

## Collaborations and Cross-Cultural Partnerships

Collaborating with international podcasters, creators, and media outlets is a strategic approach to expanding international reach and fostering cross-cultural exchange. Joint productions, co-hosted episodes, guest appearances, and cross-promotional campaigns enable podcasters to tap into each other's audiences, leverage mutual networks, and gain exposure in new markets. Collaborations also offer opportunities for knowledge sharing, creative synergy, and cross-pollination of ideas, enriching the podcasting landscape with diverse perspectives and voices from around the world.

## Global Distribution and Platform Accessibility

Leveraging podcasting platforms and distribution networks with global reach is essential for reaching international audiences effectively. Podcasters should ensure their content is accessible across popular platforms and directories worldwide, including Apple Podcasts, Spotify, Google Podcasts, Stitcher, and regional platforms catering to specific markets. Optimizing metadata, tags, and keywords in multiple languages improves discoverability and search visibility, enabling international audiences to find and engage with podcast content seamlessly. Additionally, considering local regulations, data privacy laws, and platform preferences is crucial for compliance and accessibility in different regions.

## Audience Engagement and Community Building

Building a global audience requires proactive audience engagement and community building efforts. Podcasters can engage with international listeners through social media platforms, online forums, virtual events, and community-driven initiatives. Encouraging listener feedback, conducting listener surveys, and hosting live Q&A sessions facilitate two-way communication, foster audience interaction, and cultivate a sense of belonging among international listeners. Creating dedicated online communities, fan clubs, and social media groups enables podcasters to connect with fans worldwide, share exclusive content, and foster a vibrant global community around their podcast.

## Cross-Promotion and Amplification

Cross-promotion and amplification strategies are instrumental in reaching international audiences and expanding brand visibility. Podcasters can collaborate with influencers, content creators, and media outlets in target markets to amplify their reach and attract new listeners. Guest appearances on international podcasts, participation in industry events, and media partnerships provide opportunities for exposure, networking, and audience acquisition. Leveraging social media influencers, local ambassadors, and brand advocates facilitates word-of-mouth marketing and viral sharing, driving engagement and growth in international markets.

Expanding international reach requires a strategic approach, cultural sensitivity, and proactive engagement with diverse audiences worldwide. By embracing localization, cultural adaptation, collaborations, global distribution, audience engagement, and cross-promotion, podcasters can reach new audiences, foster global connections, and position themselves for success in the dynamic and competitive landscape of international podcasting.

# 11.4 Ethical Considerations in Podcasting

———

In the ever-evolving landscape of podcasting, ethical considerations play a crucial role in shaping the integrity, credibility, and impact of podcasts. This section explores the ethical dimensions of podcasting, including transparency, authenticity, inclusivity, and responsible content creation.

Podcasting, as a powerful medium for storytelling and communication, carries ethical responsibilities that podcasters must navigate to uphold trust, integrity, and ethical standards. Whether creating narrative-driven podcasts, interview-based shows, educational content, or journalistic endeavors, podcasters face ethical dilemmas and challenges that require thoughtful consideration and ethical decision-making. Here are key ethical considerations in podcasting:

**Transparency and Disclosure**

Maintaining transparency and disclosure is paramount in podcasting to build trust and credibility with audiences. Podcasters should clearly disclose any conflicts of interest, sponsorships, affiliations, or paid endorsements to listeners, ensuring transparency in content creation, monetization, and promotional activities. Providing transparent information about sources, research methods, and editorial decisions enhances accountability and integrity, enabling audiences to make informed judgments and engage with content responsibly.

**Authenticity and Integrity**

Upholding authenticity and integrity is fundamental in podcasting to preserve the trust and loyalty of audiences. Podcasters should prioritize honesty, accuracy, and authenticity in storytelling, narration, and interviews, avoiding misleading or deceptive practices that compromise credibility. Maintaining editorial independence, fact-checking information, and verifying sources are essential practices to uphold journalistic integrity and ethical standards.

Striving for authenticity fosters meaningful connections with listeners, cultivates audience loyalty, and distinguishes podcasts as trusted sources of information and entertainment.

## Inclusivity and Representation

Promoting inclusivity and representation is essential in podcasting to amplify diverse voices, perspectives, and experiences. Podcasters should embrace diversity, equity, and inclusion principles in content creation, guest selection, and storytelling, ensuring representation of underrepresented communities, marginalized voices, and diverse viewpoints. Prioritizing inclusive language, cultural sensitivity, and diverse representation fosters empathy, understanding, and social cohesion, enriching the podcasting landscape with diverse narratives and contributions that reflect the complexity of human experiences.

## Privacy and Consent

Respecting privacy and obtaining consent are critical ethical considerations in podcasting, particularly in interview-based shows, personal storytelling, and sensitive topics. Podcasters should obtain informed consent from guests, participants, and individuals featured in episodes, respecting their rights to privacy, confidentiality, and autonomy. Protecting personal information, sensitive data, and confidential conversations is paramount to avoid breaches of privacy and trust. Implementing clear consent processes, privacy policies, and ethical guidelines ensures ethical conduct and compliance with legal and ethical standards regarding data protection and privacy rights.

## Responsible Content Creation

Practicing responsible content creation involves exercising ethical judgment, empathy, and social responsibility in podcasting. Podcasters should be mindful of the potential impact of their content on audiences, communities, and society at large, avoiding harm, misinformation, and sensationalism. Ethical storytelling involves contextualizing narratives, avoiding exploitation, and prioritizing the well-being and dignity of individuals featured in episodes. Engaging in responsible content creation contributes to a culture of ethical journalism, media literacy, and informed public discourse, empowering audiences to navigate complex issues critically and responsibly.

## Accountability and Feedback

Embracing accountability and feedback is integral to ethical podcasting, enabling podcasters to address mistakes, rectify errors, and learn from constructive criticism. Podcasters should be open to feedback, accountability, and dialogue with audiences, acknowledging their responsibility to rectify inaccuracies, clarify misunderstandings, and address listener concerns promptly. Establishing mechanisms for audience feedback, corrections, and retractions demonstrates a commitment to accountability, transparency, and continuous improvement, strengthening trust and credibility in podcasting.

## Community Engagement and Social Impact

Fostering community engagement and social impact underscores the ethical dimension of podcasting as a platform for civic engagement, advocacy, and social change. Podcasters have the opportunity to use their platform to raise awareness, amplify marginalized voices, and catalyze positive social impact initiatives. Engaging with listeners, community organizations, and advocacy groups enables podcasters to address social issues, promote dialogue, and mobilize collective action toward positive change. Leveraging podcasting for social good aligns with ethical principles of social responsibility, civic engagement, and public service, empowering podcasters to make meaningful contributions to society.

Ethical considerations in podcasting encompass a range of principles and practices that uphold trust, integrity, and responsible content creation. By embracing transparency, authenticity, inclusivity, privacy, responsible content creation, accountability, community engagement, and social impact, podcasters can navigate ethical challenges, uphold ethical standards, and contribute to a vibrant, ethical podcasting ecosystem.

# 11.5 Your Ongoing Podcasting Journey

---

In the rapidly evolving landscape of podcasting, navigating your ongoing podcasting journey requires adaptability, innovation, and a strategic approach to stay relevant and successful. This section explores strategies for continuous growth, sustainability, and success in your podcasting endeavors.

As you embark on your ongoing podcasting journey, it's essential to adopt a proactive mindset, embrace learning opportunities, and continuously refine your approach to podcasting. Here are key strategies and considerations to guide your ongoing podcasting journey:

## Continuous Learning and Skill Development

Podcasting is a dynamic field with evolving trends, technologies, and best practices. Commit to continuous learning and skill development by staying updated on industry trends, attending conferences, workshops, and webinars, and seeking mentorship from experienced podcasters. Invest in expanding your podcasting skills, such as audio editing, interviewing techniques, storytelling, marketing, and audience engagement strategies, to enhance the quality and impact of your podcast.

## Audience Feedback and Iteration

Your audience is a valuable source of insights, feedback, and ideas for improving your podcast. Actively solicit feedback from listeners through surveys, social media polls, and direct communication channels to understand their preferences, interests, and suggestions. Use audience feedback to iteratively improve your content, format, and production quality, ensuring that your podcast remains engaging, relevant, and responsive to audience needs and preferences.

## Strategic Growth and Expansion

Strategically plan for the growth and expansion of your podcast by setting clear goals, benchmarks, and milestones to track your progress and success. Identify opportunities for audience growth, market expansion, and monetization, such as exploring new content formats, collaborating with influencers, or launching spin-off podcasts. Leverage data analytics, audience insights, and market research to inform strategic decisions and investments that align with your long-term vision and objectives for your podcasting journey.

## Monetization and Sustainability

Explore diverse monetization strategies and revenue streams to sustain and grow your podcasting venture. Beyond traditional advertising and sponsorships, consider options such as merchandise sales, premium content subscriptions, crowdfunding, live events, and affiliate marketing partnerships to diversify your revenue sources and enhance financial sustainability. Prioritize building strong relationships with sponsors, advertisers, and supporters based on trust, mutual value, and alignment with your brand and audience.

## Community Building and Engagement

Cultivate a loyal and engaged community around your podcast by fostering meaningful connections, interactions, and conversations with your audience. Create opportunities for listener engagement, participation, and collaboration through Q&A sessions, live events, social media groups, and exclusive content offerings. Empower your listeners to become advocates, ambassadors, and contributors to your podcasting community, driving organic growth, word-of-mouth referrals, and long-term sustainability.

## Resilience and Adaptability

The podcasting landscape is characterized by constant change, challenges, and disruptions. Cultivate resilience and adaptability as essential qualities to navigate uncertainties, setbacks, and unexpected developments in your podcasting journey. Embrace experimentation, innovation, and flexibility in your approach to content creation, distribution, and audience engagement, allowing you to pivot, iterate, and evolve in response to evolving trends, technologies, and audience preferences.

## Personal Growth and Fulfillment

Your podcasting journey is not only about achieving external success but also about personal growth, fulfillment, and creative expression. Reflect on your motivations, values, and aspirations as a podcaster, and prioritize self-care, balance, and well-being in your pursuit of podcasting excellence. Celebrate milestones, achievements, and moments of creative inspiration, and stay connected to your passion, purpose, and joy in podcasting as you continue to grow and evolve in your journey.

Your ongoing podcasting journey is a dynamic, multifaceted adventure filled with opportunities, challenges, and discoveries. By embracing continuous learning, audience feedback, strategic growth, monetization, community building, resilience, and personal fulfillment, you can navigate your podcasting journey with confidence, creativity, and resilience, unlocking new horizons and realizing your vision for podcasting excellence.

# Chapter 12: Podcast Promotion and Marketing

Podcast promotion and marketing are essential components of growing your audience and increasing the visibility of your podcast. In this chapter, we'll delve into various strategies and tactics to effectively promote your podcast and develop a robust marketing plan.

# 12.1 Building a Promotional Strategy

———

Building a promotional strategy for your podcast involves careful planning, understanding your audience, and leveraging various channels to reach potential listeners. Here are key steps to develop an effective promotional strategy:

### Understanding Your Audience

Before diving into promotional activities, it's crucial to have a deep understanding of your target audience. Conduct thorough research to identify their demographics, interests, preferences, and pain points. This information will help you tailor your promotional efforts to resonate with your audience effectively.

### Setting Clear Goals

Define clear and specific goals for your podcast promotion efforts. Whether you aim to increase listenership, drive website traffic, generate leads, or enhance brand awareness, setting measurable objectives will guide your promotional strategy and help you track progress.

### Crafting Compelling Messaging

Develop compelling messaging that communicates the value proposition of your podcast and captures the attention of your target audience. Craft concise and engaging copy for promotional materials such as social media posts, email newsletters, website content, and podcast descriptions. Highlight what sets your podcast apart and why listeners should tune in.

### Utilizing Multiple Channels

Leverage a diverse range of promotional channels to maximize your podcast's reach and exposure. Explore social media platforms like Twitter, Facebook, Instagram, LinkedIn, and TikTok to share engaging content, interact with your audience, and promote new episodes. Additionally, consider email marketing, guest blogging, influencer partnerships, and collaborations with other podcasters to expand your audience reach.

## Optimizing for Search Engines

Ensure your podcast is discoverable online by optimizing it for search engines. Use relevant keywords in your podcast title, description, episode titles, and metadata to improve its visibility in search results. Submit your podcast to popular podcast directories and platforms such as Apple Podcasts, Spotify, Pocket Casts, and Podbean to enhance its discoverability.

## Engaging with Your Audience

Actively engage with your audience across various channels to foster community and build relationships. Respond to listener comments, messages, and feedback promptly. Encourage audience participation through Q&A sessions, polls, surveys, and listener-generated content. Cultivate a sense of belonging and loyalty among your listeners by making them feel heard and valued.

## Creating Shareable Content

Develop shareable content that encourages listeners to spread the word about your podcast. Create visually appealing graphics, audiograms, teaser videos, and highlight clips from your episodes to share on social media platforms. Encourage listeners to share these snippets with their networks, amplifying your podcast's reach and attracting new listeners.

## Monitoring and Analyzing Performance

Monitor the performance of your promotional efforts using analytics tools and platforms. Track key metrics such as website traffic, social media engagement, podcast downloads, listener demographics, and conversion rates. Analyze this data regularly to evaluate the effectiveness of your promotional tactics and make informed decisions to optimize future campaigns.

## Adjusting and Iterating

Remain flexible and adaptive in your approach to podcast promotion. Continuously evaluate the performance of your promotional activities and be willing to adjust your strategy based on insights and feedback. Experiment with different tactics, channels, and messaging to identify what resonates most with your audience. Iterate on your promotional strategy to refine and improve results over time.

By following these steps and implementing a well-crafted promotional strategy, you can effectively market your podcast and attract a larger audience of engaged listeners. Remember to stay consistent, authentic, and responsive to your audience's needs and preferences as you promote your podcast across various channels and platforms.

# 12.2 Leveraging Social Media Platforms

═══

Social media platforms offer powerful tools for promoting your podcast, engaging with your audience, and expanding your reach. Leveraging these platforms effectively can help you attract new listeners, foster community engagement, and increase the visibility of your podcast. In this section, we'll explore strategies for leveraging various social media platforms to promote your podcast effectively.

**Understanding Social Media Platforms**

Before diving into social media promotion, it's essential to understand the unique features, demographics, and best practices of different platforms. Each social media platform has its strengths and audience preferences, so tailor your approach accordingly. Common platforms for podcast promotion include:

❖ **Facebook:** With over 2 billion active users, Facebook offers extensive reach and diverse targeting options through its advertising platform. Create a Facebook Page for your podcast to share updates, engage with your audience, and join relevant groups or communities to promote your content organically.

❖ **Twitter:** Twitter is a fast-paced platform ideal for real-time engagement and conversations. Use hashtags to increase the visibility of your tweets and participate in relevant conversations within your niche. Share episode announcements, behind-the-scenes content, and engage with listeners and influencers in your industry.

❖ **Instagram:** Instagram is a visual-centric platform perfect for showcasing your podcast's personality and brand. Use Instagram Stories, IGTV, and Reels to share engaging video content, audiograms, and behind-the-scenes glimpses of your podcasting process. Leverage hashtags and location tags to reach new audiences and encourage user-generated content through interactive features like polls and Q&A sessions.

❖ **LinkedIn:** LinkedIn is a professional networking platform where you can share thought leadership content, network with industry professionals, and promote your podcast to a business-oriented audience. Publish articles, participate in relevant LinkedIn Groups, and connect with potential guests or collaborators in your niche.

❖ **YouTube:** YouTube offers opportunities to repurpose your podcast episodes into video content or create supplementary videos such as interviews, tutorials, or highlight reels. Create a YouTube channel for your podcast, optimize video titles and descriptions with relevant keywords, and engage with your audience through comments and community posts.

❖ **TikTok:** As one of the fastest-growing platforms, TikTok offers immense potential for viral growth through short, engaging video content. Create attention-grabbing clips from your podcast, participate in trending challenges, and use TikTok's powerful algorithm to reach new audiences. Authenticity and creativity are key to standing out on TikTok, so focus on creating content that resonates with your podcast's tone and style.

❖ **Snapchat:** Snapchat's focus on ephemeral content makes it a great platform for real-time engagement. Use Snapchat Stories to share exclusive previews of upcoming episodes, behind-the-scenes content, and personal interactions. Filters, stickers, and lenses can also help you craft interactive and engaging content that connects with younger audiences.

## Crafting Engaging Content

Regardless of the platform, focus on creating engaging and valuable content that resonates with your audience. Share teaser clips, episode highlights, quotes, and visual content to pique curiosity and encourage listeners to tune in to your podcast. Experiment with different formats, storytelling techniques, and multimedia elements to keep your social media content fresh and captivating.

## Consistency and Frequency

Consistency is key to building a strong presence on social media. Develop a content calendar and posting schedule to maintain regular activity and keep your audience engaged. Experiment with different posting frequencies and times to identify the optimal cadence for reaching your audience. Strike a balance between promotional content, behind-the-scenes glimpses, audience interactions, and curated content relevant to your niche.

## Engaging with Your Audience

Actively engage with your audience on social media by responding to comments, messages, and mentions promptly. Foster two-way conversations, ask questions, and encourage feedback to build relationships and foster community engagement. Show appreciation for your followers by acknowledging their contributions, sharing user-generated content, and featuring listener testimonials or shoutouts.

## Utilizing Paid Advertising

Consider incorporating paid advertising into your social media strategy to amplify your reach and target specific audience segments. Platforms like Facebook Ads, Instagram Ads, Twitter Ads, and LinkedIn Ads offer robust targeting options to reach users based on demographics, interests, behaviors, and engagement with your content. Experiment with different ad formats, objectives, and audience targeting criteria to optimize your advertising campaigns for maximum effectiveness.

## Measuring Performance and Optimization

Track the performance of your social media efforts using platform analytics and third-party tools to assess engagement, reach, clicks, conversions, and other key metrics. Analyze which types of content resonate most with your audience and adjust your strategy accordingly. A/B test different content formats, messaging styles, and visuals to identify what drives the best results. Continuously optimize your social media strategy based on data insights and audience feedback to maximize the impact of your promotional efforts.

By leveraging social media platforms strategically and engaging with your audience authentically, you can effectively promote your podcast, expand your reach, and cultivate a loyal listener base. Experiment with different platforms, content formats, and engagement tactics to find what works best for your podcast and audience.

# 12.3 Cross-Promotion with Other Podcasts

———

Cross-promotion with other podcasts can be a highly effective strategy for expanding your audience, increasing brand awareness, and building relationships within the podcasting community. By collaborating with other podcasters, you can leverage their existing audience to attract new listeners to your show and vice versa. In this section, we'll explore how to effectively execute cross-promotion campaigns and maximize their impact.

**Identifying Potential Partners**

Start by identifying podcasts that share a similar target audience or niche as yours. Look for podcasts with complementary content or themes that align with your own podcast's topics and interests. Consider reaching out to podcasters who have a similar audience size or engagement level to ensure a mutually beneficial partnership.

**Initiating Collaboration**

Once you've identified potential partners, reach out to them with a personalized and professional pitch outlining the benefits of collaborating. Highlight how your podcasts complement each other and why cross-promotion would be valuable for both parties. Offer specific ideas or proposals for how you can promote each other's shows, such as guest appearances, shoutouts, or co-branded content.

**Collaborative Content Ideas**

There are various ways to collaborate with other podcasts and create engaging cross-promotional content. Some collaborative content ideas include:

★ **Guest Appearances:** Invite podcast hosts or guests to appear on each other's shows as guest speakers or interviewees. This allows you to tap into each other's audiences and provide valuable insights or expertise on relevant topics.

★ **Shoutouts and Endorsements:** Give shoutouts to each other's podcasts during your episodes or include endorsements in your show notes or social media posts. This can help introduce your audience to other podcasts they might enjoy and vice versa.

★ **Cross-Promotional Episodes:** Collaborate on special episodes or series where you co-host or feature segments from each other's podcasts. This allows you to leverage each other's content and provide additional value to your listeners.

★ **Joint Events or Giveaways:** Organize joint events, contests, or giveaways where listeners can participate and win prizes from both podcasts. This encourages engagement and interaction between your audiences while promoting both shows simultaneously.

## Creating Coordinated Promotion Plans

Coordinate your cross-promotion efforts with your partners to ensure consistency and maximize impact. Develop a shared promotion plan outlining the timing, messaging, and channels for promoting each other's podcasts. This could include social media posts, newsletter mentions, website banners, and other promotional assets. Align your messaging and branding to create a cohesive cross-promotional campaign that resonates with both audiences.

## Tracking Results and Evaluation

Monitor the effectiveness of your cross-promotion efforts by tracking key metrics such as website traffic, social media engagement, subscriber growth, and listener feedback. Use tracking links or promo codes to attribute incoming traffic or new subscribers to specific cross-promotion initiatives. Evaluate the success of your campaigns based on these metrics and adjust your approach accordingly for future collaborations.

## Building Long-Term Relationships

Cross-promotion is not just a one-time activity but an ongoing opportunity to build lasting relationships within the podcasting community. Nurture your relationships with other podcasters by continuing to support and promote each other's shows, collaborating on future projects, and participating in industry events or networks. By fostering genuine connections and partnerships, you can create a supportive ecosystem that benefits all parties involved.

Cross-promotion with other podcasts can be a mutually beneficial strategy for expanding your audience, increasing brand visibility, and fostering relationships within the podcasting community. By identifying compatible partners, collaborating on engaging content, coordinating promotion efforts, and tracking results, you can leverage the power of cross-promotion to grow your podcast and connect with new listeners.

# 12.4 Utilizing Email Marketing

---

Email marketing remains one of the most effective and direct ways to engage with your audience, promote your podcast, and nurture relationships with your listeners. In this section, we'll explore how you can leverage email marketing strategies to grow your podcast audience, increase listener engagement, and drive traffic to your episodes.

### Building an Email List

The foundation of any successful email marketing strategy is a quality email list comprised of engaged and interested subscribers. Start by implementing opt-in forms on your podcast website, blog, or social media channels to capture email addresses from your audience. Offer incentives such as exclusive content, bonus episodes, or giveaways to encourage sign-ups. Segment your email list based on audience interests, preferences, or behavior to deliver more personalized and targeted messaging.

### Creating Compelling Email Content

When crafting your email content, focus on providing value, relevance, and authenticity to your subscribers. Share updates, behind-the-scenes insights, and exclusive content related to your podcast to keep your audience engaged and informed. Consider including teaser snippets or highlights from recent episodes to entice subscribers to listen. Use compelling subject lines, clear calls to action, and visually appealing design elements to optimize open rates and click-through rates.

### Automating Email Campaigns

Take advantage of email automation tools and workflows to streamline your email marketing efforts and deliver timely, relevant messages to your subscribers. Set up automated welcome emails to greet new subscribers and introduce them to your podcast. Create drip campaigns to nurture leads and guide subscribers through the listener journey, from discovery to engagement to conversion. Utilize triggers and segmentation to deliver targeted emails based on subscriber actions or interests.

### Promoting Episodes and Content

Use email marketing to promote your podcast episodes, highlight featured guests, and share valuable content with your subscribers. Send out regular newsletters or episode alerts to notify subscribers of new releases and encourage them to listen. Include links to your podcast episodes, show notes, and related resources to make it easy for subscribers to engage with your content. Experiment with different email formats, such as roundup emails, curated playlists, or themed collections, to keep your messaging fresh and engaging.

### Encouraging Listener Engagement

Foster two-way communication and interaction with your audience through email marketing. Encourage subscribers to reply to your emails with feedback, questions, or suggestions for future episodes. Incorporate polls, surveys, or quizzes to gather insights and preferences from your audience. Create opportunities for subscribers to participate in contests, challenges, or exclusive events to deepen their connection with your podcast community.

### Analyzing Performance and Optimization

Track and analyze key metrics such as open rates, click-through rates, conversion rates, and unsubscribe rates to measure the effectiveness of your email marketing campaigns. Use A/B testing to experiment with different subject lines, content formats, and calls to action to optimize engagement and conversion rates. Monitor subscriber engagement and feedback to identify trends, preferences, and opportunities for improvement in your email marketing strategy.

### Maintaining Compliance and Best Practices

Ensure compliance with email marketing regulations such as the CAN-SPAM Act and GDPR to protect subscriber privacy and avoid potential legal issues. Obtain explicit consent from subscribers before sending marketing emails and provide clear opt-out mechanisms to honor their preferences. Follow best practices for email deliverability, including maintaining a clean email list, avoiding spam triggers, and adhering to email service provider guidelines.

Email marketing is a powerful tool for podcast promotion and audience engagement, allowing you to connect with your listeners on a personal level and drive traffic to your episodes. By building a quality email list, creating compelling content, leveraging automation, promoting your episodes, encouraging engagement, analyzing performance, and maintaining compliance, you can harness the full potential of email marketing to grow your podcast and cultivate a loyal audience.

# 12.5 Collaborating with Influencers and Partners

———

Collaborating with influencers and strategic partners can significantly amplify your podcast's reach, enhance credibility, and attract new listeners. In this section, we'll explore how to identify, approach, and collaborate with influencers and partners to promote your podcast effectively.

## Identifying Potential Influencers and Partners

Start by identifying individuals or organizations in your niche or industry who have a significant following, authority, or influence within your target audience. Look for influencers and partners whose values, interests, and audience align with your podcast's content and objectives. Consider influencers across various platforms such as social media, blogs, YouTube, or other podcasts.

## Research and Outreach

Conduct thorough research to understand the influencer or partner's background, content, audience demographics, engagement metrics, and previous collaborations. Personalize your outreach efforts by demonstrating genuine interest in their work and highlighting how collaboration can benefit both parties. Be clear about your podcast's value proposition, target audience, and goals for the collaboration.

## Building Relationships

Focus on building authentic and mutually beneficial relationships with influencers and partners based on trust, respect, and shared interests. Engage with their content, provide meaningful feedback, and offer support before and after pitching collaboration ideas. Invest time in nurturing relationships through networking, collaboration opportunities, and ongoing communication.

## Creating Collaborative Content

Collaborate with influencers and partners to create compelling and engaging content that resonates with your shared audience. Explore various collaboration formats such as guest interviews, co-hosted episodes, joint events, sponsored content, or cross-promotional campaigns. Align the content themes, messaging, and formats to ensure relevance and authenticity.

## Amplifying Reach and Engagement

Leverage the influence and reach of your collaborators to amplify your podcast's visibility, reach, and engagement. Encourage influencers and partners to promote your podcast episodes, share your content with their audience, and participate in cross-promotional activities. Utilize their platforms, networks, and channels to reach new listeners and expand your podcast community.

## Measuring Impact and ROI

Track and measure the impact of your collaborations in terms of audience growth, engagement metrics, website traffic, social media mentions, and podcast downloads. Use tracking links, referral codes, or custom promo codes to attribute traffic and conversions generated through influencer and partner collaborations. Analyze the ROI of each collaboration to evaluate its effectiveness and inform future partnership strategies.

## Maintaining Transparency and Integrity

Maintain transparency and integrity in your collaborations by clearly disclosing any sponsored content, paid partnerships, or affiliate relationships to your audience. Ensure that collaborations align with your podcast's values, mission, and editorial integrity to maintain credibility and trust with your listeners. Avoid partnerships that compromise your authenticity or dilute your brand identity.

## Fostering Long-Term Partnerships

Prioritize building long-term relationships with influencers and partners based on mutual trust, respect, and shared goals. Explore opportunities for ongoing collaborations, recurring guest appearances, or co-branded initiatives to deepen the partnership and maximize impact over time. Invest in nurturing and nurturing these partnerships to foster sustainable growth and success for your podcast.

Collaborating with influencers and partners can be a valuable strategy for promoting your podcast, expanding your audience, and enhancing your brand's visibility and credibility. By identifying potential collaborators, conducting thorough research, building authentic relationships, creating collaborative content, amplifying reach and engagement, measuring impact and ROI, maintaining transparency and integrity, and fostering long-term partnerships, you can leverage the power of influencers and partners to achieve your podcasting goals effectively.

# Chapter 13: Audience Interaction and Engagement

Engaging with your audience is crucial for building a loyal community around your podcast. In this chapter, we'll delve into various strategies and tactics to foster interaction and engagement with your listeners, turning passive listeners into active participants.

# 13.1 Creating Interactive Content

Interactive content offers a dynamic and engaging way to involve your audience in your podcast. By incorporating interactive elements into your episodes, you can encourage participation, spark conversations, and deepen connections with your listeners. Here are several strategies for creating interactive content:

**Interactive Q&A Sessions**

Host live Q&A sessions where listeners can submit their questions in real-time via social media platforms, email, or dedicated Q&A forums. Respond to their queries during the episode, addressing their concerns, sharing insights, and providing valuable advice. Encourage audience participation by promoting upcoming Q&A sessions in advance and soliciting questions from your audience.

**Audience Polls and Surveys**

Conduct polls and surveys to gather feedback, insights, and preferences from your audience on various topics related to your podcast. Use polling features on social media platforms, email newsletters, or dedicated survey tools to collect responses. Share the results and insights from the polls during your episodes, discussing key findings and insights with your audience.

**Interactive Storytelling**

Invite listeners to contribute to the storytelling process by sharing their personal anecdotes, experiences, or perspectives related to your podcast's theme or topic. Incorporate listener stories into your episodes, highlighting their voices, and experiences. Encourage listeners to submit their stories via email, voicemail, or dedicated story-sharing platforms.

**Live Events and Meetups**

Organize live events, meetups, or virtual gatherings where listeners can connect with you and fellow fans in person or online. Host live recordings, panel discussions, workshops, or Q&A sessions during these events, providing opportunities for direct interaction and engagement with your audience. Promote upcoming events on your podcast, website, and social media channels to encourage attendance.

### Interactive Games and Challenges

Introduce interactive games, quizzes, challenges, or contests that encourage audience participation and engagement. Create fun and engaging activities related to your podcast's theme or niche, encouraging listeners to participate and compete for prizes or recognition. Share updates, leaderboard rankings, and winners' announcements during your episodes to maintain excitement and momentum.

### Community Engagement Platforms

Establish dedicated community engagement platforms such as forums, social media groups, or online communities where listeners can connect, interact, and engage with each other between episodes. Foster a supportive and inclusive community environment where members can share ideas, discuss topics, ask questions, and collaborate on projects related to your podcast.

### Listener Feedback and Contributions

Encourage listeners to share their feedback, suggestions, and contributions to your podcast by providing multiple channels for communication such as email, voicemail, social media, or dedicated feedback forms. Acknowledge and appreciate listener input by featuring their comments, questions, or testimonials in your episodes, creating a sense of belonging and ownership among your audience.

### Engagement Challenges and Initiatives

Launch engagement challenges, initiatives, or campaigns that encourage listeners to take specific actions, participate in activities, or share content related to your podcast. Set clear goals, guidelines, and incentives for participation, rewarding listeners for their engagement and contributions. Keep the momentum going by promoting ongoing challenges and initiatives regularly.

Creating interactive content is an effective way to foster audience interaction and engagement, transforming passive listeners into active participants in your podcasting journey. By incorporating interactive Q&A sessions, audience polls and surveys, interactive storytelling, live events and meetups, interactive games and challenges, community engagement platforms, listener feedback and contributions, and engagement challenges and initiatives, you can cultivate a vibrant and engaged community around your podcast, driving listener loyalty, retention, and advocacy.

# 13.2 Hosting Live Q&A Sessions and Events

Hosting live Q&A sessions and events offers a direct and interactive way to engage with your audience in real-time. These sessions provide an opportunity for listeners to ask questions, share their thoughts, and connect with you on a more personal level. Here are several strategies for hosting successful live Q&A sessions and events:

### Selecting the Right Platform

Choose a platform that aligns with your audience's preferences and accessibility. Popular options include social media platforms like Instagram Live, Facebook Live, Twitter Spaces, and YouTube Live, as well as dedicated webinar platforms like Zoom and Crowdcast. Consider the features, audience reach, and technical requirements of each platform before making your decision.

### Promoting Your Event

Promote your live Q&A session or event across multiple channels to maximize visibility and participation. Utilize your podcast episodes, website, email newsletter, and social media platforms to announce the event, share details, and encourage listeners to mark their calendars. Create visually appealing graphics, teaser videos, and countdown posts to generate excitement and anticipation.

### Setting a Clear Agenda

Define a clear agenda and purpose for your live Q&A session or event to guide the discussion and keep participants engaged. Determine the topics or themes you'll cover, establish ground rules for participation, and outline the format and duration of the session. Communicate the agenda and expectations to your audience in advance to ensure everyone is on the same page.

### Engaging Your Audience

Encourage audience participation and interaction throughout the session by inviting listeners to ask questions, share their experiences, and contribute to the discussion. Use interactive features like polls, chat rooms, and Q&A tools to facilitate engagement and solicit feedback from participants. Acknowledge and respond to audience comments, questions, and contributions in real-time to create a dynamic and inclusive atmosphere.

**Preparing Your Content**

Prepare relevant and engaging content to share during the live Q&A session or event. Create presentation slides, visuals, or multimedia content to support your discussion and illustrate key points. Practice your delivery and anticipate potential questions or topics that may arise during the session. Be prepared to adapt and improvise based on audience feedback and interaction.

**Managing Technical Aspects**

Test your equipment, internet connection, and streaming setup in advance to ensure everything is functioning smoothly. Familiarize yourself with the features and controls of the platform you'll be using, such as audio and video settings, screen sharing options, and participant management tools. Have a backup plan in place in case of technical glitches or disruptions.

**Following Up After the Event**

Follow up with participants after the live Q&A session or event to maintain engagement and foster ongoing connections. Share a recap of the event highlights, key takeaways, and resources discussed during the session. Express appreciation for attendees' participation and feedback and invite them to join future events or continue the conversation on other platforms.

Hosting live Q&A sessions and events is an effective way to engage with your audience in real-time, foster meaningful connections, and provide value to your listeners. By selecting the right platform, promoting your event, setting a clear agenda, engaging your audience, preparing your content, managing technical aspects, and following up after the event, you can create memorable and impactful experiences that strengthen your relationship with your audience and enhance the overall success of your podcast.

# 13.3 Encouraging User-Generated Content

User-generated content (UGC) is a powerful tool for fostering engagement and building community around your podcast. By encouraging your audience to create and share their own content related to your podcast, you can amplify their voices, strengthen their connection to your brand, and enrich the overall listening experience. Here are several strategies for encouraging user-generated content:

## Establish Clear Guidelines

Provide clear guidelines and instructions for creating and sharing user-generated content. Clearly define the types of content you're seeking, such as listener stories, reviews, testimonials, artwork, memes, videos, or social media posts. Specify any relevant themes, topics, or hashtags to use when sharing content related to your podcast.

## Promote Call-to-Actions

Promote call-to-actions (CTAs) across your podcast episodes, website, social media platforms, and email newsletter to encourage listeners to create and share user-generated content. Use engaging language and visuals to inspire participation and convey the value of their contributions. Incorporate CTAs into your podcast intros, outros, and episode descriptions to reach a wider audience.

## Highlight User Contributions

Recognize and showcase user-generated content on your podcast and other digital channels to celebrate your audience's creativity and engagement. Share listener stories, reviews, artwork, or testimonials during your podcast episodes, and give credit to the creators. Feature user-generated content on your website, social media profiles, and email newsletter to amplify their voices and inspire others to participate.

## Create Challenges or Contests

Launch challenges, contests, or campaigns to encourage listeners to create and share user-generated content based on specific themes or prompts. Offer incentives, prizes, or rewards to incentivize participation and generate excitement. Examples include art contests, storytelling challenges, meme competitions, or photo/video challenges related to your podcast topics or brand.

## Foster Community Engagement

Create opportunities for your audience to engage with each other and collaborate on user-generated content. Establish dedicated social media groups, forums, or online communities where listeners can share their creations, interact with fellow fans, and provide feedback. Encourage peer-to-peer engagement and facilitate connections among your audience members.

## Provide Resources and Support

Provide resources, tools, and support to help your audience create high-quality user-generated content. Offer tips, templates, or guidelines for content creation, such as photography tips, writing prompts, or design resources. Share tutorials, behind-the-scenes insights, or creative inspiration to spark ideas and empower your audience to express themselves.

## Engage in Conversation

Actively engage with user-generated content by liking, commenting, and sharing posts created by your audience. Respond to comments, questions, or feedback to show appreciation for their contributions and foster a sense of community. Use storytelling techniques to connect with listeners on a personal level and encourage further participation.

## Monitor and Moderate Content

Monitor user-generated content to ensure it aligns with your brand values and community guidelines. Moderate comments, posts, or submissions to maintain a positive and inclusive environment for your audience. Address any inappropriate or off-topic content respectfully and transparently and provide guidance on how to improve future contributions.

## Measure Impact and Iterate

Track the impact of user-generated content initiatives by monitoring metrics such as engagement, reach, sentiment, and participation rates. Analyze which types of content resonate most with your audience and adjust your strategies accordingly. Solicit feedback from your audience to understand their preferences and continuously improve your approach to encouraging user-generated content.

## Collaborate with Influencers and Partners:

Collaborate with influencers, brand ambassadors, or partners to amplify your user-generated content initiatives and reach a broader audience. Partner with influencers who align with your podcast niche or target demographic to co-create content, host joint challenges or contests, or cross-promote each other's content. Leverage their expertise, reach, and credibility to increase visibility and engagement.

Encouraging user-generated content is an effective strategy for fostering audience interaction and engagement, building community, and enhancing the overall success of your podcast. By establishing clear guidelines, promoting call-to-actions, highlighting user contributions, creating challenges or contests, fostering community engagement, providing resources and support, engaging in conversation, monitoring and moderating content, measuring impact and iterating, and collaborating with influencers and partners, you can empower your audience to become active participants in shaping the narrative of your podcast and contribute to its growth and success.

# 13.4 Building Online Communities

———

Building an online community around your podcast can significantly enhance audience interaction, foster deeper connections among listeners, and create a sense of belonging. Online communities provide a platform for like-minded individuals to engage, share experiences, and support each other, contributing to a vibrant and active fan base. Here are strategies for building and nurturing online communities for your podcast:

**Choose the Right Platform**

Select the appropriate platform(s) for hosting your online community based on your audience demographics, preferences, and communication style. Common platforms include social media networks (e.g., Facebook Groups, Twitter Chats), forums (e.g., Reddit, Discourse), messaging apps (e.g., Discord, Slack), and dedicated community platforms (e.g., Mighty Networks, Circle). Consider the features, privacy settings, moderation tools, and user experience offered by each platform.

**Define Community Guidelines**

Establish clear and comprehensive community guidelines outlining the rules, expectations, and values for participation within your online community. Define acceptable behavior, content guidelines, moderation policies, and consequences for violations. Communicate the guidelines prominently to members and enforce them consistently to maintain a positive and inclusive environment.

**Encourage Active Participation**

Encourage active participation and engagement within your online community by facilitating discussions, asking questions, and soliciting feedback from members. Share thought-provoking topics, conversation starters, or exclusive content to spark conversations and encourage members to contribute their insights, experiences, and opinions. Recognize and celebrate members who actively participate and contribute value to the community.

## Foster a Sense of Belonging

Foster a sense of belonging and camaraderie among community members by creating opportunities for connection, collaboration, and mutual support. Facilitate introductions, icebreaker activities, or networking events to help members get to know each other and build relationships. Encourage empathy, kindness, and inclusivity within the community to ensure that all members feel welcome and valued.

## Provide Value-Added Content

Provide value-added content, resources, or perks exclusively for community members to incentivize participation and reward loyalty. Offer access to behind-the-scenes content, exclusive interviews, bonus episodes, early access to episodes, discounts on merchandise, or special events as incentives for joining and engaging with the community. Regularly update the community with relevant news, updates, and exclusive opportunities to maintain interest and engagement.

## Cultivate Community Leaders

Identify and nurture community leaders, advocates, or moderators who can help facilitate discussions, resolve conflicts, and uphold community guidelines. Empower these individuals to take on leadership roles, moderate discussions, and foster positive interactions within the community. Provide training, support, and recognition for community leaders to encourage their continued engagement and commitment.

## Implement Effective Moderation

Implement effective moderation practices to maintain a safe, respectful, and constructive environment within your online community. Monitor discussions, comments, and user-generated content to ensure compliance with community guidelines and address any inappropriate behavior or content promptly. Use moderation tools, filters, and reporting systems to manage spam, trolls, or disruptive members effectively.

### Organize Community Events

Organize community events, meetups, or virtual gatherings to facilitate real-world connections and strengthen the sense of community among members. Host live Q&A sessions, webinars, workshops, or social events where members can interact with each other and connect with podcast hosts or special guests. Encourage members to organize their own meetups or events to foster grassroots community building.

### Solicit Feedback and Iterate

Solicit feedback from community members regularly to understand their needs, preferences, and suggestions for improving the community experience. Use surveys, polls, or feedback forms to gather input on topics, activities, features, and improvements. Act on feedback promptly and transparently, making adjustments and iterating on community initiatives based on member input to ensure that the community evolves in alignment with member needs.

### Promote a Culture of Gratitude

Promote a culture of gratitude and appreciation within the community by acknowledging and celebrating member contributions, milestones, and achievements. Recognize and thank members for their participation, support, and contributions to the community through shoutouts, awards, or special recognition. Show genuine appreciation for the diverse talents, perspectives, and contributions of community members to reinforce a positive and supportive community culture.

Building and nurturing an online community around your podcast requires careful planning, active engagement, and ongoing commitment. By choosing the right platform, defining community guidelines, encouraging active participation, fostering a sense of belonging, providing value-added content, cultivating community leaders, implementing effective moderation, organizing community events, soliciting feedback and iterating, and promoting a culture of gratitude, you can create a vibrant and thriving online community that enhances the overall listening experience for your audience and strengthens the connection to your podcast brand.

# 13.5 Implementing Listener Feedback Systems

---

Implementing effective listener feedback systems is crucial for fostering engagement, improving content quality, and building a stronger connection with your audience. By actively soliciting and responding to listener feedback, you can gain valuable insights, address audience needs and enhance the overall listening experience. Here are strategies for implementing listener feedback systems:

## Establish Multiple Feedback Channels

Offer various channels for listeners to provide feedback, including email, social media, website contact forms, voicemail hotlines, and online surveys. By providing multiple channels, you accommodate different communication preferences and make it easier for listeners to share their thoughts, questions, and suggestions.

## Encourage Open Communication

Create a culture of open communication and transparency by actively encouraging listeners to share their feedback, opinions, and ideas. Use clear and inviting language to invite feedback in podcast episodes, social media posts, website announcements, and email newsletters. Assure listeners that their feedback is valued and emphasize your commitment to listening and responding to their input.

## Regularly Request Feedback

Proactively request feedback from your audience on a regular basis to keep the lines of communication open and demonstrate your commitment to continuous improvement. Prompt listeners to share their thoughts on specific topics, episodes, guests, or segments during podcast episodes. Additionally, use social media polls, website pop-ups, and email campaigns to solicit feedback on broader themes, content preferences, and overall podcast experience.

## Provide Clear Instructions

Provide clear instructions and guidance on how listeners can submit feedback to ensure that the process is straightforward and accessible. Include contact information, submission forms, or links to feedback surveys in podcast show notes, episode descriptions, social media profiles, and website pages. Clearly communicate the types of feedback you're seeking and any specific questions or prompts you'd like listeners to address.

## Actively Listen and Respond

Actively listen to listener feedback with an open mind and genuine interest in understanding their perspectives and experiences. Regularly review feedback submissions across different channels, acknowledging receipt and expressing appreciation for each contribution. Take the time to respond thoughtfully to feedback, addressing questions, acknowledging concerns, and providing feedback on how listener input has influenced your podcasting decisions or content.

## Organize and Analyze Feedback

Organize and categorize listener feedback systematically to identify common themes, patterns, and trends. Create a centralized feedback repository or spreadsheet to track feedback submissions, categorize feedback by topic or theme, and prioritize areas for improvement. Use data analysis tools or survey software to aggregate and analyze quantitative feedback metrics, such as ratings, rankings, or scores, to identify trends and insights.

## Implement Feedback-Driven Improvements

Use listener feedback as a guide for making informed decisions and implementing improvements to your podcast content, format, and production. Identify actionable insights and opportunities for enhancement based on listener suggestions, preferences, and pain points. Experiment with new ideas, formats, or segments informed by listener feedback, and monitor the impact on audience engagement, satisfaction, and retention.

## Communicate Changes and Updates

Communicate changes, updates, or improvements resulting from listener feedback transparently and proactively to keep your audience informed and engaged. Use podcast episodes, social media announcements, website blog posts, or email newsletters to share how listener feedback has influenced your decision-making process and contributed to positive changes in the podcast. Demonstrate your responsiveness to feedback and your commitment to delivering a better listening experience for your audience.

## Foster a Feedback Loop

Foster a continuous feedback loop with your audience by closing the loop on listener feedback and keeping listeners informed of the outcomes of their input. Acknowledge and thank listeners for their feedback publicly, highlighting specific suggestions or contributions that have led to meaningful improvements. Encourage ongoing participation in the feedback process by inviting listeners to continue sharing their thoughts, questions, and ideas to shape the future direction of the podcast.

## Monitor and Iterate

Monitor the effectiveness of your listener feedback systems over time and iterate on your approach based on evolving audience needs and feedback trends. Regularly evaluate the volume, sentiment, and quality of feedback submissions to gauge audience engagement and satisfaction levels. Continuously refine your feedback collection methods, communication strategies, and response mechanisms to optimize the listener feedback experience and drive ongoing audience interaction and engagement.

Implementing effective listener feedback systems empowers you to engage with your audience, gain valuable insights, and improve your podcasting efforts continuously. By establishing multiple feedback channels, encouraging open communication, regularly requesting feedback, providing clear instructions, actively listening and responding, organizing and analyzing feedback, implementing feedback-driven improvements, communicating changes and updates, fostering a feedback loop, monitoring and iterating, you can create a dynamic feedback ecosystem that strengthens your connection with your audience and drives the success of your podcast.

**Stay Connected & Launch Your Podcast with Confidence!**

Ready to start your podcast but feeling overwhelmed? Let's make it easy for you!

Get access to our **FREE Podcasting Checklist**—a step-by-step guide to help you plan, record, and launch your podcast. From selecting the right equipment to promoting your show, this checklist covers all the essentials you need to get started.

By signing up, you'll also:

- **Join the Waitlist for Our "Build Your Podcast in 5 Days" Webinar**: Learn how to go from idea to launch with expert help—fast!
- **Be the First to Know About Our Next Book**: *Social Media Strategies for Podcasters* is coming soon, packed with tips to grow your audience and market your podcast like a pro.

Want to stay updated?

**https://start-your-podcast-already.kit.com/podcastchecklist**[1] to get access and be-in-the-know. Let's make your podcasting dreams a reality—together!

---

1. https://start-your-podcast-already.kit.com/podcast.checklist

www.ingramcontent.com/pod-product-compliance
Lightning Source LLC
Chambersburg PA
CBHW071412050326
40689CB00010B/1838